Backstage with the Original Hollywood Square

Backstage with the Original Hollywood Square

PETER MARSHALL
and Adrienne Armstrong

Foreword by Alex Trebek

RUTLEDGE HILL PRESS™

Nashville, Tennessee

A Division of Thomas Nelson, Inc.

www.ThomasNelson.com

Published by Rutledge Hill Press, a division of Thomas Nelson, Inc.,
P.O. Box 141000, Nashville, Tennessee 37214.

Letter on page 175 reprinted with the permission of Ann Landers. Letter on page176
reprinted with the permission of the estate of Henry Fonda. Letter on page 177 reprinted
with the permission of the estate of John Wayne.

Photograph Credits
Pages 10, 14 (top), 32, 38 (bottom), 40, 45, 47, 48, 53, 54, 61, 65, 66, 70, 81, 96 (bottom), 112,
119, 121, 124, 125, 127, 128, 131, 137, 139, 141, 157, 158, 172, 179, 180; color insert 1, page
5; color insert 2, page 1 courtesy of Fred Wostbrock.
Pages 14 (bottom), 29, 41, 69, 83, 115; color insert 1, page 6 courtesy of Sally Marshall.
Page 20 courtesy of Les Roberts.
Pages 22, 103; color insert 1, page 7 courtesy of Jay Redack.
Page 118 courtesy of Rev. Gabrielle Michel.
Pages 150, 152 (bottom), 153 courtesy of Adrienne Armstrong.
Page 152 (top) courtesy of Hope Murray.
All other photographs are from the collection of Peter Marshall.

Library of Congress Cataloging-in-Publication Data

Marshall, Peter
    Backstage with the original Hollywood square / Peter Marshall and Adrienne Armstrong.
        p. cm.
    Includes index.
    ISBN 1-55853-980-8
    1. Hollywood squares (Television program) 2. Marshall, Peter I. Armstrong, Adrienne
II. Title.
PN1992.77.H565 M37 2002
791.45'72--dc21   2002004960

Printed in the United States of America
02 03 04 05 06 — 5 4 3 2 1

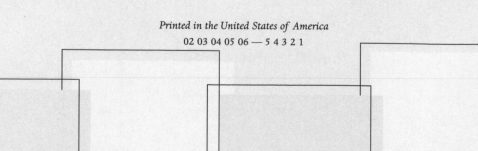

To the production staff, writers, and guest stars of
The Hollywood Squares—and especially to Merrill
Heatter and Bob Quigley, without whom the
show never would have existed

Contents

Contents

Foreword

by Alex Trebek

Why me? That was the first thing that came to mind when my friends Peter and Adrienne asked me to write this. After all, it's not as if I had a close and involved relationship with *The Hollywood Squares*. In its entire sixteen-year history on the air, I was a guest panelist for only one week and I managed to complicate things for the producers by challenging one of their rulings. After a tape stop and a short delay for some research, they reversed themselves and invited the contestant back. I, on the other hand, was never brought back, even though I continued to host *High Rollers* for Heatter/Quigley for another four years and their new production, *Battlestars*, for a year after that. So why am I being asked to write this?

As near as I can figure, it must be because, of all the people who appeared on *Squares*, I am the only one still employed in the game show area and that gives me some measure of authority and credibility. But so what? Those elements aren't necessary to get people to read this book.

In the sixties and seventies I, like everybody else, had a marvelous time each day watching Peter Marshall and his *Hollywood Squares*. The show was one half of a blockbuster hour on NBC daytime, along with a program that would come to figure prominently in my life twenty years later—*Jeopardy!* Like all great game shows, *Squares* combined the familiarity of a solid and well-known premise (the game of tic-tac-toe) with the excitement of some very funny stars and some extremely clever writing. How I envied Pete and his band of crazies! They all seemed to be having so much fun. Over the years, we the viewers got to know them all a lot better, and we came to love them as well.

Almost everyone can recall a Paul Lynde moment, a Charley Weaver smirk, a Rose Marie zinger, or a Wally Cox befuddlement. And why shouldn't they? Those were wonderful days in daytime television, and this book of memoirs will bring them all back. We are revisiting old friends on our terms.

This is our chance to enjoy the *Squares* and to go behind the scenes with Pete. You'll find out who his favorite and least favorite stars were, whether Paul was as bitchy as he sounded, and whether Charley really was a dirty old man. You might even discover why I appeared only once in sixteen years.

Acknowledgments

Writing this book took a lot of brainstorming, and we'd like to thank our dear friends who shared their stories and helped us remember ours. A special thank you to Merrill Heatter, Jerry Shaw, Art Alisi, Mary Markham and Gary Damsker, Jay Redack, Les Roberts, Harry Friedman, Lloyd Garver, Gary Johnson, Ken Hecht, Mae Quigley, Rose Marie, Karen Valentine, Abby Dalton, Nanette Fabray, Ruta Lee, Joan Rivers, Shirley Jones, Arte Johnson, and Phyllis Diller for sharing your time and your memories with us. And to Hope Murray, for giving us the impetus to begin this project.

Of course, somebody had to sell it. For this we thank the world's greatest agent, Mitch Douglas at ICM. Mitch, you're the best!

And somebody had to buy it. We thank Larry Stone at Rutledge Hill Press for his confidence in us and his enthusiasm for this book, and for giving us Jennifer Greenstein and Tracey Menges to work with. They are both absolute delights.

We'd also like to thank Dixon Hayes for his beautifully-put-together website (www.geocities.com/screenjockey) on *The Classic Hollywood Squares*. His unflagging interest in the show has inspired us. And Brendan McLaughlin, the beatmaster, who contributed most of the list of celebrity guest stars and many words of encouragement and help. Thanks also to Joe Florenski for his meticulously researched and vastly entertaining website on Paul Lynde (http://home.columbus.rr.com/paullynde/). Can't wait to read your soon-to-be-published Paul Lynde biography, Joe.

We give a very, very special thanks to Fred Wostbrock, who wrote *The Encyclopedia of TV Game Shows* with David Schwartz and Steve Rayan, for making his amazing archive of photos available to us, for sharing his extensive knowledge and love of the game show business, and for his never-ending support in this project.

■ ■ ■

I'd like to thank my dear parents, Max and Betty Richman, for always believing in me; and Kenny Adler, the man I'm going to marry, for coming back into my life and making it fun again. I'm grateful to my children, Paul, Carla, Eric, Fletcher, Brooke, and my darling Toby. Also, thanks to Peter Marshall for being the most cooperative partner in this venture and for his precious friendship of more than thirty years.

—Adrienne

I want to thank my darling wife, Laurie, who encouraged me to write this book; and my four children, Suzi, Peter, David, and Jaime, who put up with my being absent so much during their childhood and somehow ended up adoring me anyway—but not as much as I adore them. I also want to thank my managers of forty-eight years, Tom Sheils and Gloria Burke; my accountant of more than forty years, Jim Harper; and my agent, Fred Wostbrock. And Adrienne Armstrong, my talented friend, who had to sit and listen to all my drivel—and yet made sense of it all.

—Peter

Backstage with the Original Hollywood Square

A publicity photo taken before
the first show was ever taped.

Introduction

Getting to know me.

I never really wanted to write my memoirs. My wife, Laurie, has been hounding me about it for years. She thinks everything that's ever happened to me is breathtakingly interesting. "Honey," she keeps saying, "you ought to write a book." She even bought me a state-of-the-art tape recorder that has been sitting in its state-of-the-art box for more than three years. The problem is, I never really wanted to write my memoirs. So I won't. At least, not this time.

This book is about a game show called *The Hollywood Squares*. I just happen to be the guy who was lucky enough to emcee it for sixteen years.

The interesting thing about *Squares*, as we affectionately called it, was that it wasn't really much of a game. The source of its huge success was the

A backstage look at the original Hollywood Square.

George Gobel and Jonathan Winters help celebrate Mom's birthday at a *Hollywood Squares* dinner.

A studio portrait of my sister, Joanne. No wonder John Robert Powers flipped.

talented people involved, both behind and in front of the cameras. In this book, I'm going to be telling you a lot about these people, so I guess it's only fair to tell you a little bit about myself first. Don't worry. I'll be brief.

Ever since I was a kid, growing up as Ralph Pierre LaCock in Huntington, West Virginia, I knew I'd end up in show business. My dad died when I was ten years old, and we were dirt poor. Of course, I never knew that, because I didn't have anything to compare it to—everybody in West Virginia was poor. But I had something that money couldn't buy: the love and support of my mother and my sister.

By the time my sister was fourteen years old, she was drop-dead gorgeous. Mom had saved up enough money to take her to New York to see the world-famous modeling agent John Robert Powers, and he flipped. He changed her name from Letitia LaCock to Joanne Marshall (which was where I got Marshall) and she started modeling. As soon as Mom and Joanne got enough money together, they sent for me. This was the first of many times that my sister would influence my life.

I was twelve years old and had no problem adjusting to living in New

Here's Dick Haymes and my sister, Joanne, enjoying wedded bliss.

York City. In fact, I met some of the people who would figure prominently in my life there. But more about that later.

When I was fourteen, I worked nights as an usher at the Paramount Theater and when I turned fifteen, I got a job as a page at NBC. By then I was 6 feet 3 inches so they didn't have a clue how young I was, even though I weighed in at only about 110 pounds.

My ambition was to be a singer, and my sister, who by this time had changed her name to Joanne Dru and become a movie star, was married to Dick Haymes, the famous crooner.

Dick became my role model and I guess that was a good thing, because I landed my first job as a vocalist with Bob Chester at the Adams Theater in Newark, New Jersey. I continued to sing until I got drafted into the army in 1944.

When I finished my stint in the service, I returned to my singing career. Things were going okay for me, but then my sister married her second husband, John Ireland, and once again, my life changed because of her. John had a brother named Tommy Noonan, who was possibly the funniest

Entertaining the troops in Oklahoma in 1944. I kind of looked like a dart with teeth.

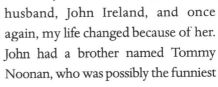

man I'd ever met. We formed an act called Noonan and Marshall and that started a whole new career for me.

Years went by, during which I got married, had four kids, and bought a big home in Woodland Hills, California. My career kept me on the road, and this caused problems between my wife, Nadine, and me. She begged me to find something that would allow me to stay at home with my family, but touring with musicals or working clubs with Tommy Noonan was the only way I knew to make a living.

Now I'm going to share a secret with you. I've always been a little psychic. I'm not saying that Dionne Warwick would hire me for her psychic hotline, but when the phone rings, I often know who it will be and what they will say. It can be more than a little disconcerting. One day, as I was packing for a working trip to New York and Nadine was all over me about it, I had an epiphany.

"Tell you what," I said. "By the time I'm forty, I'll get a game show. That will keep me close to home and everything will be fine." When I was thirty-nine, I got that game show. Let me tell you how it happened.

Noonan and Marshall's first gig was at Billy Gray's Bandbox in L.A.

1

How I Got the Job

I guess I have to thank Kellogg's cereal,
the Broadway show *Skyscraper*, and my
intense dislike of Dan Rowan.

Okay, I lied. I wasn't the very first original Hollywood Square. In 1965, one year before anyone had ever heard of the show, CBS shot a pilot starring Bert Parks. I guess they weren't completely happy with him, because they shot a second pilot with a comedian named Sandy Baron. As far as I know, CBS thought that Sandy was a little too "New Yorky" and that pilot never saw the light of day. The Bert Parks version of *The Hollywood Squares* sat around at CBS and the head of daytime television, Fred Silverman (who will come back to haunt us in this story), decided to pass. I guess he just didn't like the show.

The man who directed that pilot, Larry White, had kept track of the show, and once CBS let it go he decided to bring it over to NBC, where he was now in charge of daytime programming. Game shows were just beginning to get popular, and they were a relatively cheap form of production. We only needed one set, we paid our stars union scale, which at the time was $750 a week, and we traded prizes for a mention on the show. I don't know what they were going to pay Bert Parks, but I've got to admit that my starting salary of $1,250 a week wouldn't have broken anybody's bank.

The powers that be at NBC decided they liked the show, but Bert Parks had to go. Why, I don't know, as he was terrific in the pilot. Kind of corny, but that was Bert Parks. I guess they wanted an emcee that didn't already have a TV identity, and Bert was very well known as the master of ceremonies of *The Miss America Pageant* that was televised every year. So the great search began for a new host.

They were looking for someone who could play straight man to nine celebrities. My background was in musical comedy, but I had also been part of the successful comedy team of Noonan and Marshall. I was the Dean Martin (just not as good) to Tommy Noonan's Jerry Lewis. We had done a lot of television, including many appearances on *The Ed Sullivan Show*, and made two movies for Fox.

In 1959, we did *The Rookie,* an army spoof costarring Julie Newmar, which cost Fox $158,000 to produce. This came right on the heels of *Cleopatra*, which came in at a whopping budget of $44 million, the most expensive film made to date. This huge expenditure put Fox in major jeopardy. The lot was like a ghost town with only two shows shooting: our picture and a television series called *Adventures in Paradise*. Tommy and I would go to the commissary and the only people there would be Gardner McKay (the star of *Adventures in Paradise*), a couple of actors from his show, and a producer named Jerry Wald.

Well, the studio people told me *The Rookie* made a ton of money and helped Fox through a very tough year. It looked like a movie career was in my future.

The "Chef" bit on *The Ed Sullivan Show* upped Noonan and Marshall's price from $1,000 a week to $3,500. Pretty good money for the fifties.

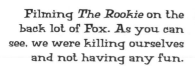

Filming *The Rookie* on the back lot of Fox. As you can see, we were killing ourselves and not having any fun.

1960. *Swinging Along* (originally released as *Double Trouble*) with Noonan and Marshall and Barbara Eden.

Julie Harris, Charles Nelson Reilly, and I are about to enjoy the last sandwich ever served at the world-famous Gaiety Delicatessen in New York, during the run of *Skyscraper*.

Fox offered us another film, *Double Trouble*, which was originally written for Martin and Lewis. It starred Barbara Eden, who would later appear many times on *The Hollywood Squares*, in her first featured role.

The movie must have been pretty bad, because even after they changed the name to *Swinging Along* and loaded it with musical stars in cameo parts, it just didn't do anything. I had gone to London to star in the stage production of *Bye Bye Birdie* with Chita Rivera the minute filming was complete and never even saw the film.

Then I got a show in New York called *Skyscraper*, with Julie Harris and Charles Nelson Reilly. After a long run, the show that was following us had to start up a little early, so I was home one week sooner than scheduled. I remember being upset because I was losing one week's salary and didn't have another gig lined up. Who could have imagined that my whole life was about to change?

Because I was home and out of work, I was receptive to the call I got from Bob Quigley. It seemed he and his partner, Merrill Heatter, had this game show and they needed a host. He invited me to audition for the job.

Legend has it that Bob's wife, Keith, was watching television when one of my Kellogg's commercials came on. She said to her husband, "That's the guy I've been trying to think of. He played straight man to Tommy Noonan. That's who you should get to host *The Hollywood Squares*." Now Quig might have just been humoring his wife, or he might have really thought that the Kellogg's guy catching all those boxes of cereal on his television set was the perfect host for his new game show. But he did call me, and because my show had closed one week early, I was home to take that call.

If all of these elements hadn't come together the way they did, I never would have found myself in the Sherman Oaks offices of Heatter/Quigley to see the pilot for their show. It was *The Hollywood Squares* starring Bert Parks and nine stars: Wally Cox, Rose Marie, Morey Amsterdam, Jim Backus, Gisele MacKenzie, Robert Q. Lewis, Charley Weaver, Vera Miles, and Abby Dalton.

"That's terrific," I said. "What a cute show. So why aren't you using Bert Parks?"

"We're looking for a complete nonentity," they told me.

"Well, look no further," I said, and they offered me an audition. Now, even though I'd told Nadine that I was going to get a game show, for some reason, I just didn't feel this was it, which just goes to show you that you can't rely 100 percent on the psychic thing. I went to the audition straight from a golf game, dressed in shorts and a T-shirt.

I should tell you that this wasn't my first crack at a game show. In 1963, I was in Las Vegas doing two musicals a night at the Thunderbird Hotel. First we'd do *High Button Shoes*, then turn around and follow it with *Anything Goes*.

This was a killer schedule and I did it for eight months. One night Noel Rubaloff, a Hollywood agent, was in the audience. He came backstage after the second performance.

"I sure hope you're being well paid," he said. "I've never seen anybody work so hard."

He was right. We were the only hotel in Vegas doing two different shows each night. When I first started, we only did *Anything Goes*, for which I was paid $1,750 a week. After four weeks, Monte Proser, the guy in charge of entertainment at the Thunderbird, decided to bring in a second show, *High Button Shoes*. I knew it was going to be a tough gig, but I was willing to do it, especially since I figured it would mean a hefty raise. When I got my first

The Las Vegas musical *High Button Shoes* was a lot of work, but it gave me a chance to dress up every night. I'm the one in the tennis shoes.

I still can't figure out which outfit looked worse—the gown from *High Button Shoes* or this getup from *Anything Goes*.

paycheck, it was $1,500. I complained to Monte that I was working twice as hard for less money and he explained it this way: "Can't be helped, kid. I've got to pay more to the band."

"You should get into daytime television," Noel told me. "You could work a few hours a week and make pots full of money."

During that time I worked nights, slept late, and had very little time for any kind of television, let alone daytime. The only thing I knew about daytime TV was that my wife sometimes watched some soap opera or other.

"Game shows," explained Noel. "I think you've got the makings of a great game show host."

I thanked him for his kind words, told him musical comedy was my life, and that was that. I continued to work very hard for not very much money.

Some time later, Noel called. He had told some producers about me and they wanted me to host a show called *Stimulus*. It was just a local celebrity game show in Los Angeles that only ran ten weeks, but it did familiarize me with the game show format. I also learned an invaluable lesson from Tom Naud, the creator of the show.

"Pete," he said, "there are going to be a lot of stars on your show—don't let them intimidate you. Just imagine that you've invited them all to a party at your home. Treat them as you would an honored guest, but always

remember—it's *your* party." This advice served me well for all the years I hosted *The Hollywood Squares,* and I never forgot it.

But back to the audition. The first thing I saw when I walked into the H-Q offices in my golf shorts was a bunch of network executives dressed in suits. In fact, that's what we called them—"suits"—because nobody else in show biz ever wears one unless they're on-camera or job hunting. The only two I can remember by name were Grant Tinker and Herb Schlosser, who had just taken over as head of NBC. I learned later that the nine people playing the stars were the Heatter/Quigley production staff, who would become so important to me as time went on. Each of them had a sign around his or her neck with names written on them: Zsa Zsa Gabor, Morey Amsterdam, Rose Marie, and so on. The acting emcee was none other than Bob Quigley, and he was the best emcee I ever saw. Bill Cullen runs a close second, but Quigley was the best. I learned so much just watching him that day.

Anyway, they gave me some questions to read and I was pretty comfortable with that, so I started feeling fairly confident about the way things were going. This went on for about twenty minutes when suddenly Merrill Heatter stopped the show—bang. "Okay, that's fine," he said.

So I went back to New York. By this time, my traveling had put such a strain on my marriage that I feared it was over. I'd met a dancer while doing *Skyscraper,* and I wanted to see her again. One morning, I got a long distance call from Bob Quigley.

"You got the job," he said. "We want you to host *The Hollywood Squares.*"

I really wasn't ready to go back to L.A., so I stalled. "Let me get my agent right on it."

I didn't have an agent for television, so I called Noel Rubaloff, who was more than happy to open negotiations. It didn't take him long to get back to me with an offer. "I don't know, I just had a meeting with Abe Burrows," I told him. "He's talking about me starring in *Breakfast at Tiffany's* with Mary Tyler Moore."

Opposite page: Four pretty good emcees: Art James, Art Fleming, Bill Cullen, and me—but Bob Quigley was still the best.

"Okay," said Noel. "But if you don't do it, they're going to hire Dan Rowan."

Now I don't dislike many people. Right now I can only think of two: Bert Convy is one and the other is Dan Rowan. Okay, okay, I know both these guys are dead, but that doesn't change the fact that I couldn't stand either of them. Tommy Noonan and I first met Dick Martin and Dan when Dick was a bartender and Dan was a used-car salesman. Dick was a great guy, friendly and funny. I've always been crazy about him and still am. Dan, however, had a snooty attitude, even then. I always felt that he thought he was better than the rest of us. Tommy introduced Dick and Dan, wrote material for them, and got them their first agent, Joe Rollo, so I guess you could say he was responsible for Dan's career. I must say that Tommy had a lot more faith in Rowan and Martin than I did. He spent a lot of time helping them with their routines and really encouraged them to stay together when things were pretty tough. Over the years, Dan pulled some pretty low tricks on us, the worst of which was taking our material without telling us or acknowledging us in any way. Tommy never let it bother him. Then Tommy got sick, really sick. I called his good friend Dan Rowan and told him that Tommy was at the Motion Picture Hospital and he was dying. Dan not only didn't come out to see Tommy, but never even picked up the phone to call. I couldn't forgive him for ignoring someone who had been nothing but a good friend, and I've disliked him intensely ever since.

I was talking about this with Dick Martin recently, and I found out that Dan had never even told him he was up for a game show. If I hadn't taken the job partly out of spite, Dan would have left Dick to host *The Hollywood Squares* and never gotten his shot on *Laugh-In.* I suppose I accidentally did Dan the biggest favor of his life when I asked my agent, "How long is the gig?"

"Thirteen weeks."

Well, I knew it would take at least that long to get the new Broadway show on its feet. "I'll do it," I said.

So I flew home to L.A. to screw Dan Rowan out of a job, and that's how I began my sixteen-year adventure on *The Hollywood Squares.*

2

The Hollywood Squares Family

The wonderful people behind the scenes of *The Hollywood Squares*.

The first thing I did when I came on board the show was have a lot of meetings with the Heatter/Quigley people. There's one thing I'd like to tell you about Merrill and Bob: they were very loyal to their employees and that loyalty was returned in kind. Most of the people I met on that first day were still there when the show ended so many years later.

To direct the show they hired Jerry Shaw, a New York director of theater and film who had been at the helm of their first show, *Video Village*. Jerry stayed with *Squares*, directing every episode until the final show from Las Vegas in 1981. Famous for running the smoothest booth in the business, Jerry worked with four cameras, while today's version of the show uses nine. He always seemed to know where to go for reactions to jokes and seldom missed the bull's-eye.

Kenny Williams, our announcer, was another *Video Village* alumnus. Kenny was a jolly fellow with ruddy cheeks and the studio audiences loved his homespun warm-ups. He always started the same way, by whispering a faint "hello." The large studio audience would completely ignore this; I'm sure most of them didn't even hear him. Then he'd bellow, "Doesn't anybody say hello when I say hello? HELLO!" The audience would yell back and the ice was broken. Another standby of Kenny's was to ask how many women in the audience had been formally introduced to their husbands. When some would raise their hands, he'd say, "The rest of you got picked up, huh?" He invariably ended with, "Two minutes to go, in case anybody has to." Believe it or not, in 1966 this was pretty racy stuff.

Enter Art Alisi. We called him St. Arthur because he was, and still is, the closest thing to a saint I've ever met. Art was one of the producers and

13

Kenny Williams did the warm-up and announce for every Heatter/Quigley show until the day he died. Now, that's a lot of announcing.

St. Art Alisi and his wife, Mary.

worked with contestants and prizes, among other things. He'd put together run-throughs for Merrill and Bob and was always finding people in need of jobs who were very capable of doing excellent work on the H-Q production staff. Whatever was needed, Art could be counted on to know how to get it.

I was watching the newest version of *The Hollywood Squares* recently, and I happened to see a contestant win more than $200,000 in cash and prizes on one show. When Arthur was in charge, his prize budget was $1,000 a week for cash, prizes, even bye-bye gifts. Of course, our contestants only earned $200 a game ($250 when the show went nighttime) and our prizes were paid for with plugs. It wasn't a big money show then, but everybody wanted to be a contestant on *The Hollywood Squares*.

Art was also in charge of the *Hollywood Squares* dinners, which became quite the thing around NBC. One of the reasons why movie, Broadway, and top television stars loved doing our show was that we always invited them to bring friends and family members to dinner. It gave *Squares* a special and warm feeling that most other shows didn't have.

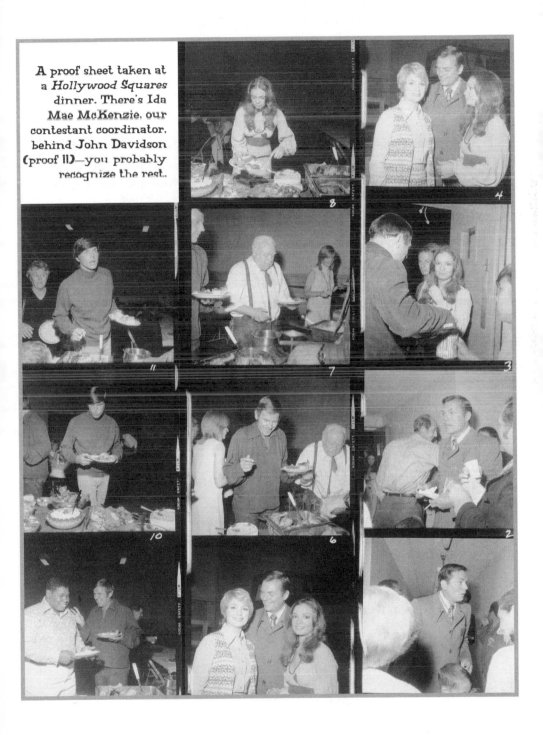

A proof sheet taken at a *Hollywood Squares* dinner. There's Ida Mae McKenzie, our contestant coordinator, behind John Davidson (proof 11)—you probably recognize the rest.

Devotees of the show never missed the Thursday and Friday episodes because they were always so much funnier. That was because we taped five shows a night and broke for dinner after Wednesday's taping. Everybody had a couple of drinks or wine with dinner and was a lot looser than on the first three shows. Art had a budget of $1,000 for catering—the same as the prize budget!

In those days, NBC was really hot. Some of the shows that taped at the same time were *The Tonight Show, The Andy Williams Show, Laugh-In, Flip Wilson,* and *The Golddiggers,* besides the specials that were always going on. It wasn't unusual to see huge stars such as Bob Hope, Frank Sinatra, Lucille Ball, George Burns, Jack Benny, and Jerry Lewis in the halls, or even sharing our makeup room. Our dinner in one of the big rehearsal halls at NBC was always full of visiting celebs, along with our own cast of stars, and I had the unexpected pleasure of breaking bread with Ed McMahon, Dean Martin, and even Frank Sinatra on one occasion. They'd walk by, see the party going

Me, being honored at a Dean Martin Roast. Do you think he was paying me back for all those free dinners?

on, and join right in. So Art made sure there was always plenty of food on hand for anyone who decided to drop in.

Our first caterer was Art's Deli, arguably the best delicatessen in the San Fernando Valley. But man does not live by deli alone, so we decided to try something a little different, a little healthier. A young butterball of a caterer showed up dressed in a green leotard. He billed himself as Richard Roughage and took great delight in jumping into the laps of the most homophobic people he could find. At that time, most folks weren't into health food, so we only used him once, and the next time I saw him he was Richard Simmons, diet and exercise guru and star of his own show.

Our cue card guy, Randy, had a girlfriend who always showed up at the studio, and when Randy asked if she could join us for dinner, of course St. Arthur said yes. This girlfriend turned out to be Debra Winger, who, coincidentally also used to work at my chiropractor's office. Small world, this show biz.

Vicki Casper came to work for the show when producer Bill Armstrong married his production secretary and they needed a replacement. She had been working with Art Alisi's wife, Mary, at the Screen Actors Guild (SAG) and Art decided that Vicki would be a prized addition to the Heatter/Quigley family. Bill walked into his office one morning and there was Miss Vicki, as she came to be known. Vicki checked him out and said, "I think you and I are going to have a much better relationship if you go downstairs and get a shoeshine."

Bill loved Vicki's take-charge attitude, and her fearless, no-nonsense demeanor made her invaluable to everyone at the office. Vicki became my liaison to Jerry Shaw. If I felt a joke was inappropriate or tasteless, I'd look at Vicki. She would backtime while I repeated the question. This allowed us to edit on air and saved countless hours and a lot of expense in the editing booth.

Art is still a schlockmeister (the guy who gets the prizes) and works with Dan Fox and Vicki Casper, just as they did when *Squares* was on the air.

Art Alisi brought Ida Mae McKenzie to the show part-time to help with the contestants. She became a full-time contestant coordinator and stayed with Heatter/Quigley for decades. She was a big woman who loved to wear bright-colored muumuus, spoke in a loud voice, and was the best charades player in the world. She treated her contestants as if they were privates in the army and she was their drill instructor, but they all loved her. To this day, whenever I run across someone who was a contestant on the show, the first thing they ask me is, "How is Ida Mae?" Sometimes, maternal Ida Mae became emotionally involved. Like the time one of the contestants was so pregnant, I thought she'd burst as she lowered herself into her seat during a commercial break.

"When is your baby due?" I asked.

"Tonight," she answered.

She had wanted to be on the show so badly, Ida Mae hadn't had the heart to kick her off. We quickly substituted players, promising the soon-to-be mom a future contestant spot on the show. I found out the next day that she never made it home. She barely got as far as St. Joseph's Hospital in Burbank, right across the street from NBC, where her baby was born.

As with most of the people who ended up on the H-Q staff, Ida Mae had been involved in show business since she was a little girl. As a child, she actually did a film with the great Charlie Chaplin. One year, Ida Mae toured with me in the summer stock production of *The Music Man*. Believe me, she never lost her theatrical flair.

An interesting side note: Ida Mae's mother had died in childbirth, and Ida Mae had been adopted by an aunt and uncle who had never told her they weren't her real parents. They also had two daughters, one the same age as Ida Mae, so they raised the two girls as twins, and Ida Mae didn't find out she was adopted until she turned fifteen. Once she learned this, she felt that she finally understood why her parents had favored her twin sister (her cousin by birth). This had caused her great emotional distress. When Ida Mae died, I spoke with this sister at the funeral. "My parents always favored Ida Mae," she told me, "because she was adopted."

Hope Berg, now Murray, also worked for Art. She was blond and cute and very, very young. At that time, I doubt if Hope had yet turned twenty-five, but she was, and still is, the smartest woman I've ever known. She recognized the possibilities of the Internet before almost anyone and has been heavily involved in that industry.

> Opposite page: That's Gary Damsker with Charo, Mary Markham sharing a square with Arte Johnson, and me doing one of my favorite things—hugging Leslie Uggams.

Using nine stars every week could have been a problem, but it seldom seemed to work out that way. Sometimes, we'd do what we called a double-taping to get ahead: we'd tape two weeks worth of shows in one week. This meant eighteen bookings, more stars than you'd have to cast in a major motion picture. To this end, Heatter/Quigley hired Mary Markham. Now Mary wasn't just a talent booker, she was *the* talent booker. In fact, before Mary, no such job existed. She suggested to Peter Potter during the run of his *Juke Box Jury* (the 1950s television show where panelists voted on whether a song was a hit or a miss) that he use stars instead of people from the audience on the panel. He agreed it was a great idea and said he would do it if *she* could convince the stars to appear on television. She did, and *Juke*

Box Jury became a huge hit. After that, if anyone wanted guest stars, they employed Mary Markham Productions to get them.

Mary was a petite blond beauty who knew everyone and was well known for her Hollywood parties. Shortly before she married the famous opera singer Lauritz Melchior, she had met a builder named Gary Damsker. She and Lauritz hired Gary to build a guest house at their Beverly Hills home while they were in Europe. By the way, that home was eventually purchased by Warren Beatty, who owns it to this day. Now that I think about it, I'm surprised Mary never talked Warren into appearing on *The Hollywood Squares*.

While Gary was building that guest house, which doubled as an office for Mary Markham Productions, he got very interested in the talent business, and after Mary's return from Europe, he became her partner. Two years after Mary's December/May marriage to Lauritz ended, she and Gary were married.

Even though she worked with so many Borscht Belt comics (even Gary is Jewish), Mary, who comes from Sedalia, Missouri, remained the quintessential WASP. I happened to overhear her talking to our producer, Bill Armstrong, about a possible booking for the next show. "I don't like him on the show," she said. "He always wants to do stick."

"That's because he's a smuck," was Bill's instant comeback.

Mary and Gary have been happily married for many years now and are enjoying a more tranquil lifestyle in beautiful Laguna Woods, California.

Les Roberts, looking like a best-selling author, in Cleveland.

During the time of *Squares,* they tackled the monumental task of booking that show with the class of Jackie Onassis and the dedication of Mother Teresa.

Let's see, who else was involved in the show? Oh, Les Roberts, Cleveland's top mystery writer, best known for the Milan Jacovich mysteries, which take place in Cleveland. He was the original line producer for the show. Les was an extremely talented writer/producer. He also was a self-taught pianist with an incredible ear. He could listen to a song once and play it like a professional, and he put this talent to good use. Whenever he wanted a little change of pace, he'd

Bill Armstrong, Archie Campbell, and me in Nashville, making *Skeedaddle*, another Marshall-Armstrong Production that didn't sell.

take a job as a piano player in an upscale cocktail lounge—also a great way to meet women.

Les Roberts left the show the second year it was on the air, and Bill Armstrong, who had been a writer, took over as producer. He became my closest friend in the world. In fact, years later, for our own production company, Marshall-Armstrong Productions, Bill and I rented the same Ventura Boulevard offices that Merrill and Bob had had when I auditioned for *Hollywood Squares*. We had some great ideas—too bad we couldn't sell any of them!

Bill was from Gloucester, Massachusetts, a small island connected to Boston by one bridge. The natives would brag that they "hadn't been over that bridge in more'n thirty years—ain't no reason to go." Bill called it Brigadoon, after the mystical town that only came to life every one hundred years. Once, while he was visiting his parents, he stopped at a little neighborhood bar and everyone was watching *The Hollywood Squares* on TV. Bill, with a little "local boy makes good" ego coming into play, was trying to figure out how to let them know who he was, when he realized they were betting on the answers to the questions. So of course he forgot about revealing his identity. Not only did he win every bet, but he even managed to astonish the New Englanders by throwing in a few of the jokes in advance. He then proceeded to spend his winnings buying drinks for everyone at the bar.

Jay Redack—now vice president of production at King World, the distributor of the latest version of *The Hollywood Squares*—also started out as a writer, then became associate producer, then coproducer. When Bill Armstrong left, he took over as line producer of the show. Jay was, and is, an extremely colorful character. He never wore socks, drove a Rolls Royce when he was making about a buck and a half a week, and had the habit of showing up at work at eleven o'clock wearing a tennis outfit. Tall and thin, with blue eyes and long curling hair, he looked like a cross between Jesus and Dudley Do-Right. Women found him extremely sexy and were always coming on to him, but Jay was happily married to a woman he adored and we could all see why. Teri Redack was a real head-turner with long, blond hair and a figure like Little Annie Fanny right out of the pages of *Playboy* magazine.

One morning, following a taping, Jay didn't show up at work. Teri called with the news that Jay had been so uptight after the show, he'd driven down to the beach to unwind. There, listening to the waves crash against the shore, he had fallen sound asleep and didn't wake up until the sun came out.

Here's Jay Redack celebrating *Hollywood Squares'* tenth anniversary with Karen Valentine.

"My poor Jay is so tired and sore, from sleeping all scrunched up like that," she told Bill Armstrong. "He can't possibly come in to work today." From that moment on Jay became known as "My Poor Jay," or MPJ for short.

Jay's sense of humor probably had more impact on the show than anyone else's. He never went for the obvious punch line. Jay would listen to the first few jokes in a pitch meeting and laugh and smile, but he'd wait until somebody came up with something totally unexpected and that became the signature of the show. "My Poor Jay" and Teri are still happily married and she has become a television writer of some note.

Les, Bill, and Jay were there at the beginning, and in my opinion, they wrote the best *Hollywood Squares* questions ever. They were three very funny guys and really enjoyed each other's humor. One time, Les was home for a week recovering from hernia surgery. Bill and Jay went to his house to lay out the show. There was Les, in his fuzzy blue bathrobe, hardly able to move because of the stitches, and Bill and Jay deliberately made him laugh so hard that his wife, Gail, finally threw them out of the house.

I'd like to talk about some of the early writers on the show, but to tell you the truth, they never stayed around long enough to get to know. I heard that Merrill and Bob went through upwards of fifty writers in the first two years. A new writer would get his two-week tryout, and Merrill would ask Les, "How's he doing?" Les would answer, "No good," and that was the end of that writer.

Ken Hecht came onboard in February 1969, his first job out of college. Ken didn't have a clue how to write a *Hollywood Squares* question and wasn't even a big fan of the show, but he was broke and really needed the job, so he tried his best. On the Friday of his second week, Ken saw Les headed down the hall and knew that his minutes as an employed person were numbered. He spent the next hour staying two steps ahead of Les. Wherever Les was, Ken wasn't. Luckily for Ken, since he couldn't possibly have kept up the dodge all day, Les got sick and went home at lunchtime. All weekend, Ken worked on writing *Hollywood Squares* questions, and somehow the light dawned. When Ken came in on Monday with pages of good questions, Les told him that if he hadn't been sick on Friday, he would have definitely gotten the boot.

Then Ken got another job but didn't tell us. He went to work on Barbara McNair's variety show, but continued to turn in his questions. Needless to say, the questions were suffering. Lloyd Garver had just moved into Ken's apartment building, fresh from Omaha, Nebraska, and was looking for a job. Ken suggested he give Heatter/Quigley a shot and even showed Lloyd how to write a *Hollywood Squares* question, which no one had ever bothered to teach him to do. Lloyd marched himself right up to the office and sure enough, they hired him—and fired Ken.

Harry Friedman, now an executive producer on *Wheel of Fortune* and *Jeopardy!*, was another writer from Omaha, Nebraska. Our show really seemed to attract them. In 1971, Harry was working in Kansas City, Missouri, but his dream was to break into television, so he gave himself a six-month deadline and moved to Los Angeles. He was hired on a freelance basis to write questions for *The Hollywood Squares* at five bucks a pop. Eventually he joined the staff as a full-time writer and became associate producer in 1973. Harry stayed with the show until production stopped in 1981.

As I mentioned before, Merrill and Bob were great employers, but they were also entrepreneurs, and Merrill was, and is, an exceptionally astute businessman for someone also so creative. For instance, he came up with a way to get a sixth nighttime show virtually for free. We always taped one full week of shows in a night, which would air from Monday to Friday. When we started doing nighttime *Squares*, we continued the practice. Then Merrill realized that, since the shows didn't air in any particular order and were only on once a week, he could throw in an extra show at every taping for very little cost. The studio, staff, catering, and hair and makeup people were all paid for, so all we had to do was give the stars a little more money. You have to admire that kind of thinking.

When the boys (that's what everybody called Merrill and Bob, but never to their faces) found out how much money they were paying every week to the composer and publisher of their theme song, they decided to publish their own music and turn a debit into a credit. In my opinion, the theme they came up with was even better than the first.

One of their money-saving ventures cost me a couple of bucks. The first version of *The Hollywood Squares* home game had my picture on the box, and I had to be paid every time one was sold or even given away as a con-solation gift on the show. That expense was taken care of by creating a new box without my picture. Easy as that.

Early on, all new writers were hired as part-timers. This meant they would submit one hundred questions a week on a trial basis. For this, they would be paid $100. If the questions were good, they would be hired to come on full-time. Lloyd Garver withstood this test, and after his two-week trial Bill Armstrong told him he was going to be hired at a salary of $175 per week. Lloyd did some quick figuring. Even though he needed the job, the numbers didn't seem quite fair. Besides, he knew that Ken had been getting $225. He told Bill that to come into the office every day, he'd have to get at least $200 a week. Bill said he'd let him know. This was on a Friday and Lloyd worried all weekend that he'd blown his chance at the job. On Monday, Bill said he'd gotten the okay to give him the $200. Years later, when Lloyd was making a more respectable salary, Bill told him he could have okayed his salary on Friday, but couldn't resist making him suffer over the weekend for his audacity.

Gary Johnson, a new writer from Omaha, had it even worse. He was hired on a trial basis at the same time as another writer. They each wrote one hundred questions for $100 a week with the promise that one of them would get a regular job. Well, it took H-Q six months to decide which one they would hire. They finally picked Gary, which turned out to be a good choice for everybody. Gary stayed with the show until the very end and is now a producer on *Jeopardy!*

When the show went nighttime, Lloyd and Gary were the only writers and they were told they would be paid an extra $100 a week. Somehow this didn't seem like very much money, but Merrill explained that only five stations had bought the show, which was true. Of course, it was an instant hit, and within four weeks was being seen in seventy-five top markets across the country, so Lloyd felt they deserved more money. Merrill's response was that if one of the markets had dropped the show and it was in four markets instead of five, he wouldn't have asked the writers to take less money.

Lloyd felt like he was getting screwed, and Merrill gave him some excellent advice. He said, "Let me tell you something about this business. If you think you're getting screwed, you probably are, but that's all we can pay for this position. If I were you, I'd try to write a good spec script and get a job on another show where you can really make some money." Three weeks later, Lloyd and Ken Hecht had their first job as a writing team on *Love*

American Style. Still feeling insecure, Lloyd kept turning in his questions for the first two weeks after he started his new job—just in case. Turned out, Lloyd worried unnecessarily. He and Ken both went on to become very big sitcom writers, each with major credits on shows such as *Family Ties; Alf; Love, Sidney;* and *Frasier.*

Another way H-Q saved some bucks was by calling our writers "editorial staff." If they'd been called writers, they would have been paid according to the Writers' Guild schedule of minimum wages, which would have been a lot more than you had to pay editorial staff. To write the questions, these guys had to devour large numbers of magazines and newspapers. They bought them, and then the bookkeeper, Gwynne Boll, would reimburse them out of petty cash. Gwynne was a middle-aged woman who still lived with her mother. She watched over Merrill and Bob's money as if it were her own and grudgingly doled out the petty cash to the guys. It seemed that each week, the receipts got bigger. Turned out that our enterprising editorial staff was picking up receipts that other customers had thrown away and turning them in as their own. Nobody could ever prove that, but when the magazine purchases soared to the same proportion as the paychecks, Gwynne started to get suspicious. Afraid of slaughtering the golden goose, they promised to cut back on magazine purchases, reducing the inflated number to something a little more realistic and not making any waves.

No one was safe from the quest to save money. Even the stars had what was called a "favored nations" clause. That meant everybody who did the show had to be paid the same, union scale, which was $750 for one week of shows, $1,250 for nighttime. In reality, nobody invoked this clause except the producers of the show, but it made it possible for many big stars to appear for very little money without losing face.

Some of our stars had their paltry salaries sent straight to other places, such as Marvin Himes Jewelers in Beverly Hills or Saks Fifth Avenue. I guess they considered it pocket change and didn't want 10 percent going to their agents, 15 percent to their managers, and 50 percent to Uncle Sam.

Once Bill Armstrong was upset with Merrill and Bob. It was during Nixon's wage freeze to control inflation in the early seventies. In television, when the network picks up a show for another season, the owners of the show, in this case Heatter and Quigley, get a substantial amount of money.

Normally, this would be shared with key employees by raising their salaries. However, when this pickup came, wages were frozen and Merrill and Bob explained to Bill, their producer, that they couldn't go against the government. So Bill had to forgo his raise until the freeze ended. Jim Brolin was going through the same thing at his show, *Marcus Welby, M.D.,* and one night at a dinner break, he and Bill decided to ask for bonuses in place of raises, but Merrill and Bob were intent on honoring the letter of the president's ruling.

After his unsuccessful meeting with his bosses, Bill stomped into the writers' office and growled to Ken and Lloyd, "I want you guys to go into the men's room and pee on the deodorant cakes—so those cheap sons of bitches will have to replace them sooner." Bill was their boss—so they did.

A couple of years later, Bill had to eat his words. He was buying a new home and hadn't sold his old house yet. Merrill and Bob generously gave him a large advance on his nighttime *Squares* salary that allowed him to make his down payment without a worry. I guess that was the last time he called his bosses cheap.

Many writers came and went over the years, and things changed pretty drastically around the office. In 1974, the show became a signatory to the Writers' Guild of America (WGA). This required their writers to join the union, so the editorial staff became real writers with better salaries and union benefits.

At that time, some of the writers were considered Q and A, and others were hired strictly for jokes. The joke writers would pitch their stuff to Jay Redack, and Jay would take the best jokes to Merrill. They would then decide which questions and jokes would be used. Learning the construction of a joke and being responsible for so many jokes a week was great training for the writers, and many of them went on to write situation comedies and sketches for comedy shows.

There was never an open line of communication between the producers and the writers, though. For instance, when a celebrity who did our show died, here's how the writer would learn about it. Someone would knock on the door and say, "No more Wally Cox questions."

Sometimes we had a show already taped, but someone on it died before it aired. Even though there was a disclaimer at the end to the effect that this show was recorded earlier, people always believed the show was happening right before their eyes. One time there were three dead people on the show at once. That must have really confused some of our viewers.

Bobby Hopper was the gofer. You know, go for coffee, go for lunch. He was an intelligent and creative young man and constantly complained about having to do all the running around. He picked up dry-cleaning, groceries, even lingerie and pantyhose for Merrill's wife, the former Elaine Stewart, all the while muttering about how he was going to somehow advance to a better position. But he did a fine job as a gofer, even though he was never happy.

One day, Merrill, Bob, Bill, and Jay were huddled in Merrill's office writing jokes so they sent Bobby out to get lunch. Bobby walked into the Cock and Bull, which was just down the street from the new H-Q offices on Sunset Boulevard in Beverly Hills, and ordered four chef's salads. The manager glanced at his watch and told Bobby he didn't take orders between 11:30 and 2:00. Now one thing Bobby did not want to do was return to the office without lunch, so he thought fast.

"You don't understand. My bosses are in a meeting with, uh, Joan Crawford, and she specifically requested your chef's salad."

Suitably impressed, the manager decided to fill the order. He put together the salads, and when Bobby offered him the company credit card, he waved it away. "No problem," said the manager. "I'll just put it on Miss Crawford's bill."

Bobby stayed with the show until the end, and after sixteen years he still held the position of gofer, but here's the success story. After the show ended, he decided to go out and try to do something more important than running other people's errands, and when Bobby decided to make a change, he made a major one. He moved to China, where he has been teaching English since 1983. From what I hear, he couldn't be happier.

I hope I haven't bored you with this list of characters from my adventure, but I know they'll be coming into the story and I'd like you to have a little background on who they are. And I loved them all so much. For many years, they really were like family to me.

3

The Genesis of
The Hollywood Squares

How Merrill Heatter and Bob Quigley's *People
Will Talk* begat *The Celebrity Game*, which begat
The Hollywood Squares.

Every family has a head of the household, and ours was the team of Merrill Heatter and Bob Quigley. Everybody called Bob "Quig" unless we were referring to the team. Then it was always "Merrill and Bob." I don't know why. That's just the way it was.

Quig had been around the business for most of his life but his career in front of the camera wasn't too successful. I think playing the Good Humor Man in TV commercials was probably the best part he ever had. He was a wonderful guy, but always fought his own private demons. When I met Quig, he was a recovering alcoholic. Once, when he was suffering from a sore throat, someone offered him cough medicine. He took a big swig, smiled, and said, "Is this stuff good for you?" And that was the closest to a drink I ever saw him get.

Merrill Heatter and Bob
Quigley, enjoying the fruits of
their labor. Incidentally, that's
Perrier in Bob's wine glass.

I did, however, see him make hundreds of bets on the ponies. I can't remember a visit to Hollywood Park or Santa Anita when I didn't see Quig there. Now Quig had a very, shall I say, distinctive way of speaking. His hands were always moving and he kind of slurred his words together and chopped off the ends. In short, he wasn't that easy to understand. One day at the races, he gave me a tip on a horse. Well, Quig was a pretty good gambler, so I took his tip to the window and made a sizable bet. Sure enough, the horse won. I sought Quig out after that race to thank him and showed him my winning tickets. Turned out, it wasn't the horse he'd tipped me on at all; I had simply misunderstood what he'd said.

In spite of his earthly vices, Quig was a Bahai priest and had spent many years in Africa with his wife, Keith, and their three children. He took a job as a disc jockey to get into Africa, and that became the excuse that allowed him to live there and spread the religious word. I'm not sure exactly why he came back—maybe life was too tough there for a young white family, or maybe he just ran out of funds. When he returned to New York, he and Keith began writing and producing game shows.

Quig became spectacularly successful and enjoyed many years on the top of the game show world. Then in the late seventies he had an accident that

really seemed to take everything out of him. He was driving in the Cheviot Hills area of Los Angeles and didn't see a motorcycle cop on his left. He turned into him by accident and the police officer died. Quig went to court on charges of vehicular homicide. He was cleared but was placed on probation. After that, things started to go downhill for Quig. He suffered from Alzheimer's, which got progressively worse until his death in February of 1989.

Merrill Heatter was the nephew of the renowned newscaster, Gabriel Heatter, and that was his introduction to the world of broadcasting. His interest in game shows, however, came from his own experience. He worked on a number of them, eventually becoming the producer of *The $64,000 Question*.

Merrill and Bob met when Quig was producing a show called *On Your Account* and hired Merrill as a writer. When that show was canceled, they became partners and tried to put together a show of their own. They came up with a couple of ideas and got some development money, but nothing really went anywhere. Then Proctor and Gamble decided to try to develop a show based on a board game with real people as the pawns. Merrill and Bob came up with *Video Village*, sold it to CBS, and that's what put them in business. Jack Narz (the brother of game show host Tom Kennedy) was the first "Mayor of Video Village"; then Monty Hall took over in that capacity. Kenny Williams was the "Town Crier," beginning his long announcing career with Heatter/Quigley Productions. *Video Village* stayed on the air for four years. During that time, the team sold another show to NBC, *Double Exposure*, hosted by Steve Dunne. Things were going great. Merrill and Bob had become the hot game show guys in New York and they were loving it. Then they got a call from NBC in Los Angeles.

"If you want to keep producing these shows, you're going to have to do it from Television City in L.A.," they were told.

For Merrill and Bob, this was not an easy decision, but if they wanted to be in the game show business, they had to be where the business was. So, kicking and screaming, they gave up their New York digs and moved to the other coast.

Opposite page: A day at the races. From left, Bob Quigley and Jerry Shaw with me and a few of Quig's other friends in the winner's circle. Quig could really pick 'em.

That move led to a cycle of shows starting with *People Will Talk* and *The Celebrity Game*, and ultimately leading to *The Hollywood Squares*. Of course many great game shows followed *Squares. Gambit, Name Droppers,* and *High Rollers* were just a few of their hits. Now Merrill, sitting in his luxurious Beverly Hills home, laughs at his reticence to leave New York as he enjoys the ultimate Southern California lifestyle.

Heatter and Quigley were the first to use a large panel of guest stars on their show *People Will Talk*. Dennis James, who later became a very close friend of mine, played host to fifteen contestants who each voted for one side of an issue such as "Is it all right to kiss in public?" or "Should bald men wear toupees?" Pretty tame stuff, but it *was* 1963. Other contestants tried to pick panel members who agreed with their opinions.

When NBC let it be known that they weren't going to renew the show, Merrill decided to try something new, hoping it might work as a sort of on-air pilot for a better version of the show that had failed. He hired Mary Markham to find fifteen celebrities who would do the show and replaced the contestant panel with the largest group of stars to ever appear on one game show. At the time, performers who did game shows were either on their way up or on their way down, so finding fifteen well-known personalities who would be willing to do the show wasn't an easy task. Mary, of course, came through with some big names, including Lee Marvin. I guess he wasn't too happy when he realized he had just done an on-the-air game show. He grabbed Merrill by the collar and said he thought he was doing a pilot. Merrill apologized for any misunderstanding and explained that the

Everybody had fun on *People Will Talk* except Lee Marvin.

show was definitely going to air. Lee put his face right in Merrill's, pulled him a little closer, grumbled something, and walked away.

The celebrity gimmick didn't work for *People Will Talk*, but it convinced Heatter and Quigley there was something to the idea of a game show with lots of stars, so they came right back with *The Celebrity Game* in 1964. Carl Reiner hosted a panel of nine who answered questions like "Do plain women make better wives than beautiful women?" or "Should a man be forced to wear a wedding ring?" The contestants tried to guess if the celebrity answered yes or no. The show aired on CBS for two five-month stints, then fizzled. I don't know why these games didn't work, but I'm sure Merrill and Bob learned a great deal in producing them that contributed to the eventual success of *The Hollywood Squares*.

Merrill was now completely preoccupied with coming up with a game that had a lot of celebrities, and he spent every Saturday morning at his home trying to figure it out. After many false starts, he took a yellow piece of cardboard and divided it into nine squares. He got photographs of nine celebrities and pasted them into the squares and took it into the office. He asked Quig what he would think if they played some sort of tic-tac-toe game and these stars had to answer questions. Well, Quig loved it—he absolutely flipped—so they concentrated on putting together a format for the show and started to shop it around. The first stop was NBC. They turned it down. Then they went to ABC, both daytime and nighttime, and *they* turned it down. At this point, Merrill and Bob started getting discouraged. If that many executives didn't see any merit in the idea of this kind of celebrity game show, maybe it just wasn't ever going to make it. And then Elliot Wax from the William Morris Agency called.

"Fred Silverman is looking for a show for CBS, and I think you ought to pitch him *The Hollywood Squares*." Merrill thought it was a big waste of time but finally agreed to a breakfast meeting. Merrill Heatter, Bob Quigley, Elliot Wax, and Fred Silverman met at the Polo Lounge at the Beverly Hills Hotel. Elliot urged Merrill to tell Silverman about the game, so Merrill grabbed a napkin and drew a tic-tac-toe board. In each square, he wrote the name of a celebrity.

"We're playing human tic-tac-toe with celebrities," said Merrill. "It's a quiz show." And Silverman said, "We'll do it. It's a deal."

Well, Merrill was smart enough to know you couldn't present this kind of show with nine people sitting on bridge chairs, so he persuaded Silverman to put up the money to build a set and make a proper presentation. In those days the cost to do this was about $80,000—a bargain compared to today's prices. The presentation was a hit and CBS agreed to make a pilot with Bert Parks. Everything looked very promising.

One night Merrill and his wife, Elaine, were in New York having dinner with none other than Fred Silverman. Fred told him he was going to put a game show on at night as a summer replacement and if it did well it would go onto the fall schedule. Merrill assumed it would be *The Hollywood Squares*, as why else would Fred be telling him this, but he assumed wrong. Silverman chose a Bob Stewart show, *The Face Is Familiar,* hosted by Jack Whittaker, which stayed on the air for six weeks. This was the first time Fred Silverman gave *The Hollywood Squares* a deathblow, but it certainly wasn't the last.

Just to give you some idea of how savvy Silverman was about game shows, when Michael Eisner was working for him, Fred had an idea of his own for a game he wanted to develop. Eisner called Merrill and Bob in to see if they could help him refine it. This was the idea: a contestant sticks his hand in an opening and feels something, then has to tell what it is.

After realizing he was really serious, Merrill said, "Mike, I'll tell you how bad this idea is, then it's your problem to tell Silverman. It will never, ever work. Even if it were fun for the person doing it, what does it mean to the viewer, and how many times can you do this before you realize the absurdity of what you're doing?" By the time Merrill and Bob left his office, Eisner was hysterical. The three of them couldn't stop laughing.

The Hollywood Squares sat at CBS for a year. By then, all rights had reverted back to Heatter/Quigley, but what were they going to do with a property that had already been turned down by all three networks?

Here's where a little bit of luck came in. Bob Quigley's good friend Larry White was an executive who had also been a director. At the time they shot the pilot for *The Hollywood Squares,* Larry was out of work. They offered him the show to direct and he jumped all over it. In this business, you have to take work where you can find it. One year later, when the show was practically dead, Larry White was once again working. He had become the head of daytime programming at NBC. Merrill and Bob took the show to him.

Now, it just so happened Merrill and Bob had another show on NBC at the time called *Showdown*, with Joe Pyne, that was about to be canceled. Larry White replaced it with *The Hollywood Squares*.

This raised more than a few eyebrows in the business and *Daily Variety* ran a full-page story on how Merrill and Bob's good friend replaced a failed show of theirs with another show they had produced. Throw in the fact that Larry had directed the pilot and it definitely smacked of insider trading, so to speak. In actuality, this wasn't the case. Larry believed in the show and was willing to put himself on the line to get it on the air.

It didn't do well at first. If you analyze the show, you can see there really isn't much of a game and in the beginning, absolutely no editing was done, unless a star misbehaved so badly it couldn't get past the network police, Compliance and Practices. Merrill didn't spot the problem, because he'd never seen the show on the air. He watched every taping at the studio and didn't think it was necessary. But he was in New York and happened to turn the show on in his hotel room. It looked painfully slow, and he realized the stars were holding the camera for as long as they could. When Merrill came back to Los Angeles, he extended the show, adding a lot of questions and

Merrill and Bob's great family of stars: From the top, Cliff Arquette (Charley Weaver), Abby Dalton, Wally Cox, Morey Amsterdam, and Rose Marie, all with me in an early publicity shot. They were the nucleus of the early shows.

editing out what he called "the garbage." We kept the show as funny as it was and managed to get in a lot more content.

Another thing Merrill and Bob knew was the importance of creating what Merrill liked to call "The Great Family of Stars." In daytime television, nothing is more important than having people on the air that the audience feels close to and wants to see more of. Mary Markham brought a lot of folks onto the show, but it was Merrill and Bob's construction that gave it its family feel and made the show what it was.

I was talking with Merrill just recently and he made an interesting comment. While he had an instinctive feeling that a game with a lot of celebrities would work, he never imagined *The Hollywood Squares* would last. His reason was that the game was weak. Unlike *Wheel of Fortune* and *Jeopardy!* —both terrific games the home audience can play along with—*Squares* is completely dependent on the gags and the tic-tac-toe gimmick is really nothing but a way to end the game.

I guess he never expected it to reap so much success and earn so many Emmys. Merrill, Bob, and Jay Redack won the award for Outstanding Game or Audience Participation Show in 1974, 1977, 1978, and 1979. Jerome Shaw won for Outstanding Individual Direction for a Game Show in 1974, 1978, and 1979. In 1973, the first year a game show ever won a writing Emmy, Jay

I gotta tell you: winning those Emmys was a great feeling.

Betty White and Allen Ludden make an appearance on the *Peter Marshall Variety Show.*

Redack, Harry Friedman, Harold Schnieder, Gary Johnson, Steve Levitch, Rick Kellard, and Rowby Goren all walked away with the coveted award. And I won Outstanding Host in a Game Show in 1973, 1974, 1979, and 1980, and Daytime Host of the Year in 1973.

That was the year I cohosted the first daytime Emmy show along with Barbara Walters. I was delighted to win the Outstanding Host Emmy that year, and I was also nominated for Daytime Host of the Year. The only other nominee was Dinah Shore. Well, I knew she would win. I mean, she's Dinah Shore! So Dinah and her producer, Henry Jaffe, were sitting in the front row of the skating rink at Rockefeller Center and it was time for the big award. Barbara Walters announced the nominees, opened the envelope, and said, "And the winner is—Peter Marshall." Dinah laughed and clapped; she'd known me since I was seventeen and I guess she figured the last thing she needed was another award, but I thought Henry was going to have a heart attack. She really was happy for me, though. She sent me a gorgeous bouquet of flowers and that really made me feel as good as winning the Emmy did.

One year I lost to Allen Ludden, but I was rooting for him all the way. I had dinner with him and his wife, Betty White, at The Rangoon Racquet Club in Beverly Hills the night before, and they kept saying that I would probably win again. The next morning, Allen and I flew to New York together. It had always astounded me that Allen had never won an Emmy, considering the wonderful work he did on *Password* for all those years. I was thrilled when his was the name that was called that year.

Another year, I lost to Richard Dawson, host of ABC's *Family Feud*. The next year, just before the winner was announced, Richard got up and started down the aisle. I guess he thought he had it knocked, but it was my name they called that time.

One year my good friend Charles Nelson Reilly was the presenter and he was positive I would win. I wasn't so sure. He said his line, "And the Emmy goes to—" then ripped open the envelope with a flourish, did a double-take, and said, *"Dick Clark?"*

The show certainly had more staying power than its creators expected. It stayed on the air for sixteen years and has been back in three different incarnations since.

Having been a part of the show for so long, I'm not really surprised that it hasn't disappeared like so many other game shows—but at the very first taping, I wouldn't have given you a Confederate dollar for its chances of lasting more than thirteen weeks.

Charlie and me with Henry Mancini. I wonder if we're drinking a toast to Dick Clark, who beat me out for an Emmy in 1978.

Merrill and Bob congratulating each other on *Squares'* tenth anniversary.

4

The Rise of
The Hollywood Squares

From a so-so beginning to the highest-rated and
longest-running celebrity game show in history.

I n the autumn of 1966, I walked into Studio 3 at NBC in Burbank for the
dress rehearsal and taping of the first week of shows of *The Hollywood
Squares*. I arrived with five brand-new suits over my arm and an ambivalent
attitude. On one hand, I was happy to have a thirteen-week gig that would
keep me in town and reestablish a little harmony at home. I was also very
happy to have screwed Dan Rowan out of a job! On the other hand, I
couldn't stop thinking about the dancer I'd met while doing *Skyscraper* and
the possibility of the lead in Abe Burrows's new musical. These things made
me anxious for the thirteen weeks to be over so I could get back to New York.

I looked up at the huge set and checked out the stars: Rose Marie, Wally
Cox, Cliff Arquette as Charley Weaver, Abby Dalton, Nick Adams, Agnes
Moorehead, Morey Amsterdam, Sally Field, and Ernest Borgnine in the
center square.

I was pretty uptight before that first taping. First of all, we only had a
couple of weeks to get ready and during most of that time I was doing the
musical *Brigadoon* with Jane Powell in Houston, so I had almost no rehearsal
time, and much of the time I did have was taken up with photo shoots and
publicity interviews.

I had to learn the opening of the show. Even today, so many years later,
I can still say this in my sleep, but in 1966, with so many other things to think
about, it wasn't that easy to do. With the help of cue cards, I managed to get
it right. Remember?

> Object for the players is to get three stars in a row either across, up and
> down, or diagonally. It is up to them to figure out if a star is giving a

correct answer or making one up. A game is worth $200. We play a two out of three match. Good luck and pick a star.

It wasn't quite as easy for me to remember which contestant was O and which was X. Finally, out of sheer desperation, I suggested we make it simple. If O was always the female contestant and X was always the male, I'd know exactly who I was talking about when I said, "Circle gets the square." One thing I never had a problem with was telling the difference between a man and a woman.

And another thing—I couldn't seem to get certain words past my fairly prominent front teeth. I started to sound like Norm Crosby doing malaprops. So I started going over the questions and writing out difficult words phonetically on my question cards. The producer, Les Roberts, always a literary type, got a good laugh when he looked over my shoulder and saw that I had written the name of the famous author of *Rebecca* as DAFF-knee doo MORE-ee-yay. But writing words that way kept me from making mistakes, or maybe I should say, from making so many mistakes. Both of these practices continued through the run of the show. With those problems out of the way, the taping of the first show went surprisingly smoothly.

Off I went to my dressing room to change for the second show, feeling a lot more confident. I was standing there in my skivvies when Merrill and Bob burst through the door. It seems I wasn't giving them what they wanted, and they were very unhappy with the job I was doing. Now, there's not a performer in the world who wouldn't be devastated upon hearing those words. I couldn't figure out if I felt hurt, defensive, or just plain pissed off. Then my life as a musical comedy actor in New York and a certain pair of long, shapely legs flashed before my eyes. I became very calm.

"Look, fellas," I said. "You hired me to do what I do and that's what I'm doing. If you want to replace me, that's fine. Just let me know when you find somebody you like better, and I'm out of here." I mustered up all the dignity I could, considering I was wearing only shorts and socks, and added, "And by the way, please don't come into my dressing room again unless you knock first."

This is about as much as I was wearing when Merrill and Bob burst into my dressing room to complain about my performance on the first show. I guess I wasn't a great emcee, but I sure had cute legs.

Opposite page: Our first taping. What a night!

They left, I took a deep breath, and went on to finish the next four shows. Unfortunately, they didn't go quite as smoothly as the first show did. It was a perfect example of Murphy's law—if anything could go wrong, it did. We had technical breakdowns, our lights stopped working, and everybody was new to the show and pretty edgy. A young production assistant moved a folding chair on the stage, and the union guy in charge of moving folding chairs threatened to lodge a formal complaint. That was worth a half-hour delay while the producers tried to get everybody calmed down. The audience, getting bored with this foolishness, started straggling out of the studio. Things kept going wrong until two in the morning, when the only people left were the ones who wanted to try out to be contestants, and even they were getting pretty surly.

When we finally finished, I went back to my dressing room and kicked off my shoes. I think I was actually glad my association with daytime television was coming to a rapid end. There was a tentative knock on my door and in came Merrill and Bob.

"That was perfect," they told me. "Exactly what we want." The funny thing is, I don't remember changing a thing from the first show. But from that moment on, we had a great relationship. I can't tell you how wonderful they were to me. Quig is gone now, but I still consider Merrill a very close personal friend. By the way, they never came into my dressing room again without knocking first.

The show debuted October 17, 1966. *The Hollywood Reporter* reviewed the first show on October 18, 1966.

> Merrill Heatter and Robert Quigley have come up with a winner in their new "Hollywood Squares" show which debuted yesterday morning. It's bright, fresh, amusing and geared to entertain the daytime viewers. This is a show for everyone—not just the housewife. It is also for the younger set who might be watching. The men will enjoy "Squares" just as much.
>
> Program is based on the familiar tic-tac-toe, with two studio contestants competing to see who gets the three marks in a row. This is done by determining whether questions asked of celebrities panelists [*sic*] are right or wrong. Format is simple, but effective.
>
> Peter Marshall is just right in the host role, looking handsome

enough for the femmes, masculine enough for any male viewer, and gracious to the contestants. He's a perfect choice for the part.

Opening show had Rose Marie, Morey Amsterdam, Abby Dalton, Wally Cox, Cliff Arquette, Ernie Borgnine, Sally Field, Nick Adams and Agnes Moorehead as the Hollywood celebs who answered the questions. Queries were of various nature, some historical, some amusing, some informative. It's fun for the homeviewer to go along with the game, too, trying to guess whether the personality is right or wrong.

And with performers like the above, the show zinged right along, never lagging. Each celeb proved capable and likeable—no "wise guys" in the box of nine. And definitely, title to the contrary, no Hollywood "squares." Rather, Hollywood sharpies. Guest panelists will be added weekly.

Directed nicely by Jerome Shaw, half-hour is definitely a winner for Heatter/Quigley and NBC. Strip show is in color, with Larry Klein program supervisor.

—Frank Barron

Although we were all delighted with the enthusiastic words of Frank Barron, nobody expected the show to last. I figured I would return to New York to do another Broadway musical and life would go on pretty much as it had. Boy, was I wrong. The show stayed on the air for sixteen years. It was a phenomenon. After a somewhat sluggish beginning, our popularity soared until we became the highest rated daytime show in history, getting 40-plus shares regularly. That means more than 40 percent of all households using television were tuned in to our show.

Not everybody loved the show. Author Charles Sopkin described his feelings about the show in his book *Seven Glorious Days, Seven Fun-Filled Nights*:

"Hollywood Squares" is tic-tac-toe, except that they use humans. A huge set fills the stage, looking something like the one in "Bye Bye Birdie," and if this doesn't fill the picture in, then let me add that the set resembles a three-tier-tic-tac-toe crossing, with "stars" sitting on each of the three tiers. And what stars, folks: Wally Cox, Glenn Ford,

Eve Arden, Charley Weaver, Kaye Ballard, Abby Dalton, Bill Bixby (remember him? I don't), Kathryn Hays (a singer, I think), and Sandy Baron, a comedian. My first nasty impulse is that the program is the brainchild of an NBC Vice President in Charge of Long-term Contracts on Stars Who Used to Be Big But Aren't Anymore. Anyhow, there they are, three stars on the bottom, three in the middle, and three on top. They're all self-conscious as hell and given to making quiet cracks to one another. "Hollywood Squares" also has another stunning innovation in the way of game shows. They've taken the troublesome business of answering questions away from the run-of-the-mill dolt who might show up as a contestant and placed the intellectual stuff in the hands of the star.

But that was one man's opinion. On May 25, 1967, *Daily Variety* announced a new rating leader, with *Hollywood Squares* getting a 35 share of the Nielsen audience.

The show became a mega-hit, so popular it actually supported prime-time television for NBC for many years. In fact, it completely overshadowed everything else I'd ever done, and I became known only as Peter Marshall, the Master of *The Hollywood Squares*.

This totally changed my life, which turned out to be a double-edged sword for me. My career as a musical-comedy performer had been really taking off when the show came my way, and I truly loved working in musical theater. My other aspirations were toward comedic acting, maybe even a situation comedy. Never once, since I started in the business at age fifteen, did I utter the words, "What I really want to be is a game show host."

But, let's face it, at that point I could have gone on doing Broadway shows for the rest of my life and only a fraction of the people who watched me every day on television would have ever seen my face or known my name. And I've got to tell you, folks, nobody goes into this business to stay anonymous. Just being associated with those nine wonderful stars every week brought a certain celebrity of its own that I still enjoy to this day, not to mention the five Emmy Awards I'm very proud to own.

And I never had to give up performing on stage. In fact, I spent twelve years singing with a talented group called The Chapter Five. We opened shows in Las Vegas, Lake Tahoe, and Reno for headliners such as Bill Cosby,

Imagine. working with all these great stars and only having to change your jacket once.

Jerry Lewis, The Mills Brothers, Joan Rivers, Dionne Warwick, Buddy Hackett, Bob Newhart, and Johnny Carson.

Without the exposure the show gave me, I never would have been considered for those kinds of bookings. And, of course, I spent part of every hiatus doing summer stock around the country, so I certainly never felt cheated out of a career in musical comedy.

When *Squares* went nighttime, this review ran in the January 15, 1968, edition of *Daily Variety*.

Television's game wardens, Merrill Heatter and Bob Quigley, are about as square as Fort Knox. They've conceived play pens for celebs with amazing success over the years and their latest brain wave turned day into night. Their matinee version has done so well NBC promoted it to the shank of the evening, hopeful it will succeed where the other tenant failed to keep up its payments to Nielsen. It's day AND night for the "squares" who come full circle for at least the rest of the season.

Game shows invariably rise or fall on the stature of the players, who like the exposure if not the emoluments. For this newest of the Heatter/Quigley syndrome, comedy will be predominant to give the show the facet of fun and phase off the questioning or the loot which sustains most of the others. Such mimics as Milton Berle and Buddy Hackett of the nine squares empaneled for the opener by Mary Markham made it more a battle of wits than a pipeline to their intellect. Questions were of the freshman type but they served only as a catalyst for the comedy. Samples: "who played the lead in 'Moby Dick'?" or "is it pronounced rarebit or rabbit?"

Peter Marshall hosts both the day and night sessions and he is a good choice—young, personable, fast on his feet or off the top of his head. Others squared in tic-tac-toe fashion were Charlie Weaver, Wally Cox, Edie Adams, Nanette Fabray, Abby Dalton, Morey Amsterdam and Raymond Burr, latter the only straight man in the pack. Basketballer Gale Goodrich played it cool while his non-pro partner in the guessing game was beyond restraint.

If "Squares" can chip away a few points from the opposing forces, and it has been done, Heatter & Quigley can chalk up another winner and stay over in the fall.

—Helm

That took care of the last remnants of game show stigma. People who never would have dreamed of doing a game show were calling us and asking to be on, all for the princely sum of $750 for the daytime show and $1,250 for nighttime, which was union scale at the time. Stars like Betty Grable, Walter Matthau, Ginger Rogers, and George C. Scott. It seemed that everybody wanted to do the show, because it was so funny.

It didn't start out that way. It was a Q and A show with a tic-tac-toe twist and questions that were written with an eye toward humor. Our clever

Wally, Abby, Cliff, and me in my favorite publicity shot of all time.

No wonder Paul
liked to call me
"Beaver Face."

regulars sometimes had cute responses to their questions, and the guest comedians could be very funny, but no one had any written jokes.

One day the writers were coming up with questions for Paul Lynde. We used to ask Paul a lot of food questions, as he was quite a gourmet, and this one happened to be about a dessert. The question was, "What's a strawberry fool?" Bill Armstrong, who was then a writer on the show said, "Wouldn't it be funny if Paul answered, 'I don't know, beaver face.'" Paul liked to call me beaver face when he got peevish. It was the first time we ever gave a panelist a joke, and it got a really big laugh. In fact, it worked out so well, we started writing joke answers to many questions.

Merrill and Bob wanted to make sure the jokes weren't too hip for the audience. Whenever a joke was written that Quig thought was too subtle, he'd say, "And then a man in a hat comes out and explains the joke to the audience." This was quickly shortened to "man-in-the-hat-joke," and we tried to avoid those as much as possible.

Some of the jokes have actually turned into classics. Probably the most famous joke from the show was quoted some years ago in an article in *Newsweek*. The question was, "Paul, why do motorcyclists wear leather jackets?" and the joke was, "Because chiffon wrinkles." Now, my ex-producer and partner, Bill Armstrong, told me he had written that joke and I always believed it until recently, when Merrill told me *he* had written it. I got in touch with Les Roberts to ask him if he remembered which of them had really written this great line, and he said, "What are you talking about? *I* wrote that joke." That made three people who each sincerely believed he had written the now-famous punch line. Determined to solve the mystery, I went to the woman who was the production secretary on the show at the time and asked if she remembered who had written the little gem.

"In a roundabout way, I did," she said, then went on to explain that Bill was having a lot of trouble finding the joke and asked her if she had any ideas. "Why do motorcyclists wear leather jackets?" She thought for a moment, then answered, "Because they don't like silk." According to her, that's what led Bill to write the much funnier, "Because chiffon wrinkles." I guess no one will ever know who really wrote the joke, but I'm glad somebody did and I'm sure Paul was, too!

These questions in the form of straight lines became known in the industry as *"The Hollywood Squares* Question." Don't get me wrong. We had other criteria for our questions besides the possible jokes. We wanted the viewer to say one of three things:

- "I knew that!"
- "That's right, it was on the tip of my tongue!"
- "Really? How interesting!"

The other possible response would be "Who cares?" and those were the questions we tried to avoid.

At the bottom of my card, I would always see some letters. These referred to the source of the question. For instance, WB meant *World Book,* LHJ meant *Ladies Home Journal,* AL meant Ann Landers, and so on. Sometimes I'd see the letters IMIU, and I could never figure out what they meant. I finally asked one of the writers, and this is what I learned. We always needed a certain number of true or false questions, and Lloyd Garver realized that if the answer to the question was false, he could make it up. Hence the IMIU stood for I Made It Up. A good example might be, "True or false? There is a popular obstetrician in Kenosha, Wisconsin, who performs all of his deliveries dressed in a stork costume." The answer, of course, was false.

Gary Johnson took the art of the IMIU question to a new level. One day, while trying to come up with some IMIUs, he decided to write a generic question about Idaho. He picked Idaho because it sounded funny to a guy from Nebraska. Let's see, he thought. Did anything of interest happen in Idaho on—and he randomly picked a date, June 5, 1976. The answer was false. Had to be. He made it up. Alas, the letters soon started pouring in from the state of Idaho. Didn't we know, they demanded, that on June 5, 1976, the huge Teton Dam collapsed, making headlines around the world? Gary is still trying to figure that one out.

But first and foremost, we had become the first written comedy game show and the funny answers were still the most important thing.

Not all the questions had joke answers, but some stars were given jokes for virtually every question they were asked. You might wonder how that could work, since the network was very strict about not allowing the stars to hear the questions before the show. How could they possibly memorize punch lines to questions if they didn't even know what the question was going to be? Well, we devised a method that allowed our entertainers to deliver hilarious one-liners that was almost foolproof.

Here's how we did it. Under my desk were nine slots. Each slot had a name that corresponded to where each star sat on the set. For instance, Paul Lynde's slot was in the middle. When Paul was called on for the first time in a show, I would take question number one from the middle slot beneath my desk. You might remember that I would say something like, "Let's go to Paul's questions" or "Here's a question for Paul." Paul would have a list in front of him and on that list were all the joke answers for that show, each with a number in front of it. I would ask Paul the question, "Does standing a five-month-old baby on his legs make him bow-legged?" Paul, glancing at joke line number one, would take a delicious pause, then answer, "No. You've got to push down on him."

Even though our writers wrote these jokes, they were made great by Paul's flawless delivery and timing. In fact, if the joke didn't work, Paul would come up with something funnier. Like the time I asked Paul this question: "Paul, who's better looking, a pixie or a fairy?" Paul, in a very masculine voice, delivered the written joke, "Looks aren't everything." But he got the really big laugh with his answer, "Oh . . . I'll go for the fairy."

Once the laughter (or laugh track, also known as Mrs. Mackenzie) died down, Paul would seriously try to give the right answer to the question or an excellent bluff. And so it went for all of our stars who got jokes, and the

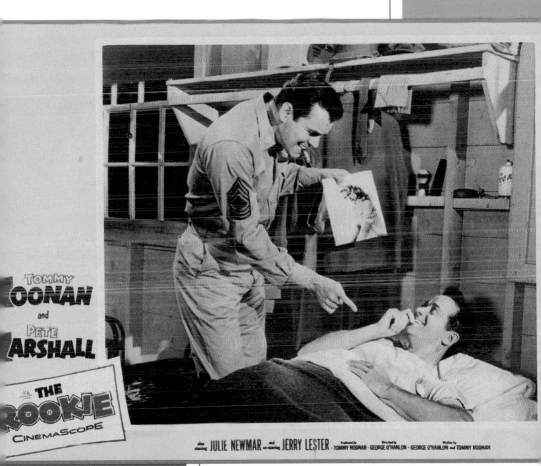

Name above the title. What a thrill!

Believe it or not, this is what got me the audition as the host of *The Hollywood Squares*.

This photo was taken before the set was even built. Art Alisi drew a bunch of tic-tac-toe games on a white background, and we went for it. Here's Wally Cox, me, Morey Amsterdam, Abby Dalton, and Rose Marie.

Both versions of *The Hollywood Squares* home game. I personally favored the first one, and so did my accountant. Incidentally, I had to buy these from e-Bay.

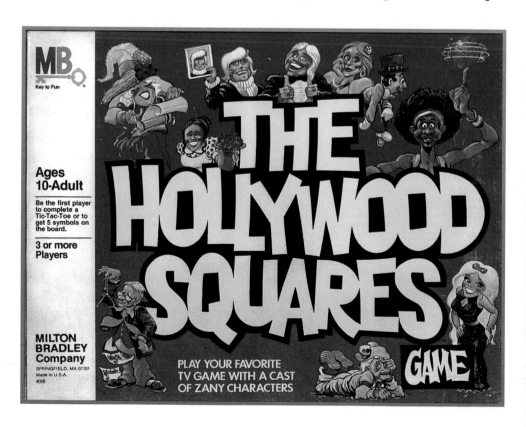

Paul could always break me up.

Here's a group shot from one of our sports theme shows. On the front of the stage are Harry Friedman and Bob Quigley (center), flanked by talent bookers. Jay is at one contestant desk and Ida Mae McKenzie at the other. In the back row on the left are a talent booker, Paul Hornung, and Burt Jones. I think the women in the middle are Jo Jo Starbuck and Janet Guthrie I just can't remember which is which. Then, on the right, are Mickey Mantle, Hank Aaron, Cathy Rigby, me, Sugar Ray Leonard, Moses Malone, and Bill Walton.

This music theme show featured Tubes, Maureen McGovern, John Stewart, Elvin Bishop, Dick Clark, the Marshall Tucker Band, England Dan & John Ford Coley, Kenny Rankin, and Seals & Crofts. As you can see, I'm not even in the photo.

Paul Lynde, George Gobel, and Harvey Korman socializing. The two guys in the background are Alex Trebek and Merrill Heatter.

Dennis James and me enjoying a gelato on the Amalfi coast—a fur piece from Huntington, West Virginia. Dennis was the host of *People Will Talk*, a predecessor of *The Hollywood Squares*.

method worked very well, even though they never knew what the question was going to be and I never knew the joke.

After a dear friend of mine and a brilliant sketch comic, who shall remain nameless, had done the show a few times, he came to me and said, "Y'know, Pete, I think I can come up with my own stuff from now on." We told him that would be fine. Well, on the first show he bombed. He didn't realize how tough it was to listen to the question, come up with a funny joke, then think of the answer or a good bluff, all in a few seconds. During the short break we took between shows, he approached me.

"Listen, Pete, maybe I could use a few of those jokes after all." He got his jokes and went back to enjoying the big laughs once again.

As I said, not all of our stars got jokes. Mel Brooks, with his brilliant comic mind, never needed any help from us. Joan Rivers also relied on her excellent comedic talents. Jay Redack and Joan were very good friends, and still are. Jay knew Joan's material so well, he could write questions that allowed her to use jokes out of her current act. Sometimes we would write jokes for Joan and she wouldn't even use them. She'd just reach into her own cache of funny stuff and come up with something a whole lot better.

Wally Cox never took a written joke. Instead, he relied on his own personality for his answers. Even so, the questions had to be written with a Wally flavor. Questions like, "Wally, how tall is your average gorilla?" would be answered with, "I don't have an *average* gorilla."

Wally knew a lot about many things; however, he knew virtually nothing about show business. Therefore, we loved to give him show-biz questions, because he always had an answer we could count on. "Wally," I would say, "Elizabeth Taylor is known to have been married many times. Who was her second husband?" Wally would answer, "Gregory Peck."

"Wally, who played opposite Spencer Tracy in *Guess Who's Coming to Dinner?*" Wally would answer, "Gregory Peck." Sometimes we'd throw in a trick question. "Wally, who was the star of *To Kill a Mockingbird?*" Wally would answer, "Gregory Peck." The contestant would disagree and be very surprised to learn Wally had the right answer—but no more surprised than Wally. This technique always worked well, and Wally Cox was one of our most popular and beloved players until his untimely death on February 15, 1973. Funny how you never forget some dates.

Sometimes Charley laughed at his own jokes, and with good reason. He'd never heard them before, either.

Charley Weaver always had jokes written for him, but sometimes he'd get called on so often we'd run out of jokes, so we always put in a few straight non-joke questions as a backup. One of them was, "Is it all right for a senior citizen to get his teeth straightened?" He replied without hesitation, "That would be my *second* choice, Peter."

No jokes were ever written for the bottom center box. We called it the lox box, or the Carol Lynley box, because that was where we usually put the pretty girl off some new television series or someone we feared might be boring. Often this person was a one-time booking and couldn't be relied upon to deliver jokes the way our pros could. This spot was also one that didn't get much action, so most of the time the star just sat there for half an hour like a lox, and that's how that particular square got its name.

I remember a sexy blond actress named Karen Jensen who was a regular on the television series *Bracken's World*. When we booked her for the lox box, Quig didn't know who she was. Of course, Quig almost never knew who the young show folk were. He watched *Bracken's World* the night before the taping, and it happened to be an episode in which she was only in one scene. When she appeared on our show, because of the mechanics of the game, she got asked four questions in a row. Quig leaned over and said, "This broad has more lines on our show than she does on her own!"

Often, every one of our nine stars was funny and bright—not a lox in the bunch. Since we always taped a week's worth of shows in one night with the same panel, we would move the panelists around, spreading the lox, so to speak.

One night Sandy Duncan was in the lox box next to Redd Foxx in the bottom left square. I watched through the taping of the first show, as Sandy's eyes got bigger and her face turned paler. I thought sure she was coming down with some form of exotic flu. Luckily, she didn't get called

Paul and I share a laugh with Totie Fields. When Redd Foxx was on the show, Totie kept him in line.

on much that show. Afterward, I immediately went over to her. "Sandy, are you okay?"

Now, Redd was a raunchy old guy and nothing seemed like more fun to him than teasing innocent little Sandy. Turns out that all during the show, he was bombarding her with sexual innuendoes that I can't even begin to repeat here. He did everything he could think of to provoke her, short of flashing. At least, I don't think he flashed—but he might have. I checked out the set. "Don't worry about a thing," I told Sandy.

During the fifteen-minute break between shows, I asked if the star from the upper middle box would switch seats with Sandy, and when we came back, Redd found himself sitting next to Totie Fields, who was famous for giving back as good as she got and then some. For the next four shows, I watched as Redd became more and more subdued. I never dared to ask Totie what she did to keep Redd on his best behavior, but I must admit that I sometimes entertain myself thinking about it.

Sometimes, we would put more than one star in a square. Sonny and Cher shared a square, as did three members of The Monkees and all four of The Lennon Sisters, two per box.

We'd take people from the same show, like Conrad Bain and Dana Plato from *Different Strokes*, and put them right into one little box. We did the same with relatives like Donny and Marie Osmond.

Donny and Marie look like they should be in *Hair*.

And on our theme shows, like soap operas or sports, we had two people in almost every box.

Once I got two people in a box that I didn't expect. I went to Wally with a question and heard an unexpected voice. I looked up to see Arte Johnson, who had wandered over from a *Laugh-In* taping across the hall and climbed into the square with Wally. They looked like two little munchkins as they debated the answer to the question.

One of the highlights for our studio audience, and for me, I might add, was when Dino, Desi, and Billy shared a square. They were a singing group in the seventies made up of Dino Martin Jr., Desi Arnaz Jr., and Billy Hinsche. Proud mom Lucille Ball showed up at the taping. Lucy strode on to the set with her flaming red hair and piercing blue eyes, and a hush fell over the studio audience—it was like a visit from the queen. She took one look at her baby boy, crammed into a square with his singing partners, and her eyes blazed.

She approached the producers and demanded that Desi get his own square. Now, Lucy had a lot of power and she wasn't used to hearing the word "no," but all the other squares were full, so what could we do? Fortunately, nobody told Lucy that Merrill and Bob never would have given those boys their own squares anyway. She turned on her heel and left the set on those gorgeous long legs of hers, the power of speech returned to the audience, and the show went on. I guess I don't need to add that it was the last time we saw Dino, Desi, and Billy on our show.

As television changes from year to year, so did our regulars and semi-regulars. Karen Valentine, JoAnne Worley, and Alan Sues all joined our family. Lily Tomlin, Marty Allen, Mickey Rooney, Phyllis Diller, Michael Landon, and Gypsy Rose Lee made frequent appearances. I've often wished I could see all those stars again, but it was common knowledge that NBC had erased the original tapes to save space and money. When I got wind of the fact that they didn't want to store the tapes anymore, Jerry Shaw, Art Alisi, and I tried to buy them, but by the time we got there with our offer, we were told the shows had already been destroyed.

Now, this was one of the great mysteries of the twentieth century to me, because recently, over three thousand tapes have been found and on April 15, 2002, they began airing on the Game Show Network. Where have these tapes been all these years? Who found them? Was it somebody's master plan to hide them, à la Jackie Gleason with the lost *Honeymooners* tapes, or did they somehow just slip out of sight?

The Monkees, JoAnne Worley, Judy Carne, Henry Gibson, and me. The long and the short and the very short of it.

Arte Johnson loved being on *Squares,* even when he hadn't been booked.

I started doing a little investigating, and this is what I learned. In 2001 Jim Pierson of Dan Curtis Productions was searching through a media storage warehouse in Burbank for some old episodes of *Dark Shadows* and came across shelves and shelves of two-inch quad masters, a format that hasn't been used in many years, labeled *The Hollywood Squares*. These were original shows with the NBC labels on them going all the way back to 1968 and into the late seventies. At the time, Jim, David Schwartz (one of the authors of *The Encyclopedia of TV Game Shows*), and Cary Mansfield were producing a CD of game show theme music so Jim mentioned it to David, who also happens to work for the Game Show Network. David went to the folks at GSN, who contacted MGM, the current owners of *The Hollywood Squares*. It seems that even though the accounting department had been paying the storage bills since they acquired the show, they had no idea what they had. You could call it inheritance confusion. Over the years, the property had gone from Filmways, who had made copies of the shows and had them stored, to Orion, who did absolutely nothing with the stuff, to MGM in the nineties. By then, what with so many acquisitions and the turnover of personnel, nobody knew they were there. At first, MGM simply denied that these shows existed, but Jim Pierson was able to show them exactly where they were. That's when the Game Show Network and MGM struck their deal.

Now we'll all be able to see these shows again. I know they'll only reinforce the stories that stand out in my mind and the wonderful friendships that I will never forget.

5

Three Squares a Day

An in-depth look at Wally Cox, Cliff Arquette
(Charley Weaver), and Paul Lynde.

Wallace Maynard Cox
December 6, 1924–February 15, 1973

> *Q:* Is James Stewart his real name?
>
> *Wally:* Is James Stewart whose real name?

Remember when I told you that some of the people I met when I moved to New York as a kid would play a part in my later life? Well, Wally Cox was one of them. Wally was one year ahead of me at PS 165, which was located at 109th Street in Manhattan. We shared a common hatred for our French teacher, an imposing German woman named Mrs. Blanchenstein, but other than that we had very little in common.

Flash forward. New York, 1950. My partner, Tommy Noonan, was dating a girl named Pocahontas Crowfoot, whom he eventually married, and she had a roommate named Shirley Ballard. Shirley was one of the prettiest things you'd ever seen, so I spent a lot of time at that apartment. Now, I wasn't the only one sniffing around Shirley. Robert Horton used to come around and so did a young actor named Marlon Brando, whose roommate and best friend was Wally Cox

Wally wasn't in show business; he was a silversmith, a dance instructor, and anything else that allowed him to earn a buck, but he used to do great impressions. Not of stars, but of people he'd met. I remember one he did of a guy he met in the service called Dufoe, that crazy guy Dufoe. Some of these impressions turned into monologues, and they were so good that Brando talked him into joining the American Creative Theater Group, where he put together a nightclub act. In December of 1948, he auditioned for the owner of the Village Vanguard and was hired to perform that very night. This one-night stand turned into a six-month stint that led to more clubs, a Broadway revue, and many TV and radio appearances. By 1951, Wally had his own radio show in New York and accepted a starring role in NBC's *Philco Television Playhouse* production of *The Copper*. From this role as a mild-mannered, trouble-prone policeman, producer Fred Coe developed a sitcom pilot just for him. Wally became a huge star, but he always hated being called Mr. Peepers, even though the show was the catalyst for his suc-

Wally—it was never quite the same without him.

cess. I think he preferred being known as the voice of Underdog, a role that always impressed my kids.

Wally was small in stature, wore horn-rimmed glasses, and came to the studio on a Harley-Davidson the size of a small truck. In all the years we taped the show, he never wore anything except his rumpled brown suit during the daytime tapings and the same black suit for the nighttime shows. Appearances weren't a really high priority with Wally, but people were. I've been talking to a lot of my old, dear friends since I started writing this book, and one of the questions I ask is, "Who was your best friend on the show?" Rose Marie, Nanette Fabray, and Abby Dalton all answered "Wally Cox," without a moment's thought.

Wally was a brilliant, multitalented individual who not only made his mark in show business but was also a master builder. He had a home on the East Coast that he had actually built from the ground up. He did the electricity, the plumbing, the whole nine yards. When I moved into my home in Encino, I couldn't figure out the wiring. My outside lights stayed on for six months because I couldn't find the switch to turn them off. Wally dug into it and not only figured out where every wire went, but he also rewired a lot of the old work and drew a plan so that no one would ever have to face that problem again.

He was also an avid rock hound. I spent some of my favorite Saturday mornings in the hills of Agoura with Wally. The area, just west of the San Fernando Valley, was not too developed at that time and we were able to find some beautiful and rare rocks that we took to Wally's house and put into his rock polisher. I gave most of those specimens to my kids, but I still have a few that are among my most cherished possessions.

Wally grew up a tormented child, a product of a broken home. His father was a military man and somewhat of a tyrant when it came to raising his son. His parents' closest friends, also in the military, had a son about the same age as Wally. He considered Wally his best friend, but Wally had another take on it. Whenever little Marlon Brando came over to play, Wally would try to hide or come down with some mysterious illness. But Marlon always loved Wally. In fact, at Wally's wake we all looked for Marlon, who was nowhere to be seen. Word finally filtered around that he was locked up in Wally's guesthouse, inconsolably grieving the loss of his friend. Nothing too odd about that, except for the fact that Marlon, who was quite large, was said to be wearing tiny Wally's pajamas.

After the divorce of Wally's parents, he was raised by his mother, the mystery writer Eleanor Blake, who had entered into a lesbian relationship long before it was considered an alternative lifestyle. While he was happier with his new set of nontraditional parents than he'd ever been with his natural father, this unusual living arrangement left Wally with some psychological issues that kept him on the couch for his entire adult life.

He often told me not to get involved in this kind of therapy unless I was willing to stick with it forever. The saddest thing was, after spending years being psychoanalyzed, Wally learned he had a chemical imbalance that had been the root of his psychological problems. Wally began drug therapy and I believe this is what ultimately killed him. You see, he also suffered from arteriosclerosis and Wally did enjoy a drink now and then. His death was diagnosed as a heart attack brought on by a lethal mix of prescription pills and liquor. There was a rumor going around that Wally had committed suicide, but I have a very good reason for not buying into that theory.

Wally had a real vendetta against the phone company and had finally convinced our producer, Bill Armstrong, to allow him to rewire the telephones in Bill's home so that all his long-distance calls would be free. Wally bragged that he hadn't paid for a long-distance call in years. He died before he ever finished the job. Now, I knew Wally, and when he had a mission, there's no way he'd let anything get in his way until the mission was accomplished. Wally never would have committed suicide until he'd finished cheating the telephone company out of every possible penny. That's how I know his death was an accident. Somehow, this knowledge gives me comfort, although I miss him to this day.

Cliff Arquette as Charley Weaver
December 28, 1907–September 23, 1974

> Q: What do most dentists say you should do with your dentures when you go to bed?
>
> Charley: Out at the home, we throw them into the center of the room and have a swap party.

Here's Cliff reading a letter. I guess it must be from Mama.

Most of you will remember Cliff as the folksy character he invented, Charley Weaver. He gained national fame in the fifties, reading his "Letters From Mama" on the *Jack Paar Show*. In fact, his book, *Charley Weaver's Letters From Mama*, became a national best-seller.

I met Cliff when I was about eighteen. He was doing the Autolite Radio Show with my brother-in-law, Dick Haymes. In those days, radio shows were played to a live audience, so you had to dress in full costume. Since there were no satellites or delayed broadcasts, they would do one show for the East Coast, then three hours later, do an identical show for the West Coast. Well, Cliffie played Dick's mother, Mrs. Wilson, on the show, and he did it in full drag. Between shows, Cliff would get bored, so he would go out for a couple of drinks. Then he'd sit in his car on Hollywood Boulevard, still dressed in full old-lady drag. Even though the war was over,

I always loved Cliff, but it looks like he preferred Marty Allen.

the town was full of soldiers and sailors. Cliff would wait for one or two to walk down the street, then he'd jump out of his car and say, "Hey, sailor. Want to have a good time?" Now, I have to tell you, Cliff looked like an apparition. The young servicemen would run for their lives, sometimes calling the cops and complaining. The police would just shrug and say, "That's Cliffie again."

And he always loved the ladies. For many years, he was particularly enamored of a certain lady of the evening. Those were the days of key clubs, or wife-swapping. Cliff's favorite thing to do was to hire his lady for the night. They would go to a key club in Redondo Beach pretending to be a married couple, and then he would swap her for somebody else's wife. During that time, Cliff had intimate relationships with half the young housewives in the South Bay, and many husbands enjoyed the services of Cliff's date without ever knowing they were in the company of a very expensive professional.

Cliff and Wally were very close; in fact, they used to share a dressing room and the oddest thing happened after Wally's death. I already mentioned that Wally was a real whiz with electricity. Well, shortly after he died, the lights in Cliff's square started to do strange things. They would flicker for no apparent reason. The electricians would try to fix it, but it would just keep happening. Then the lights would go out completely, but only in Cliff's box. After about a month of this, I suggested that the stagehands just leave Cliff in the dark. Clearly, Wally wanted it that way. Shortly after that, it stopped happening as quickly as it started.

Cliff had a very serious stroke, and none of us thought he would even recover. He did, but he was sick, not at all like the old Cliff. Merrill and Bob brought him back to the show as soon as he was physically able to do it. Believe me, this took a lot of courage on their part. Most people in this business won't touch anybody who's been ill or who is even suspected of being ill. But, as I've told you, Merrill and Bob had a great deal of loyalty to the people who worked for them. So they brought Cliff back. Unfortunately, he wasn't as sharp as he had been. He'd lost a ton of weight and his Charley Weaver outfit hung on him. I think he lost some memory, too, because suddenly Cliff didn't know the answers to any questions, and this was all stuff he had always known before. That's when we bent the rules a little and started helping him with his answers. If we hadn't, he would have looked stupid and ruined his reputation as an intelligent man and a Civil War expert. Like with one question—I can't remember exactly what it was, but let's pretend it was something simple like, "Who accepted the surrender at Appomattox, Grant or Lee?" Obviously the answer was Grant, but the writer accidentally wrote down Lee. Since we didn't have a research staff, nobody checked the answer. It went all the way down the chain of command and nobody caught the mistake. Now, the question gets on the show. Cliff answers, "Robert E. Lee." I look at the card and there it is, "Robert E. Lee." Now how the heck could anybody believe that Cliffie would give that answer, so blatantly wrong, unless somebody had given him the answer and he was too out of it to know the difference? I can't remember how we got out of that one, but somehow we did. As time went on, Cliff started to get better, and he worked right up until the time of his death from a massive stroke.

I think one of the nicest things Bob and Merrill ever did was for Cliff. Unfortunately, it happened after his death and he never knew about it. For many of his later years, Cliff was keeping company with a woman named Miriam. When he died, he neglected to make any provision for her and without him, she was destitute. Merrill and Bob put her on the payroll so she could continue to live as comfortably as she did when Cliff was alive.

By the way, all those Arquettes you keep hearing about are Cliff's grandchildren. Rosanna, Patricia, David, Richard, and Alexis have all proven themselves as actors. It makes me feel so good to see Cliff's legacy live on.

Paul Lynde
June 13, 1926–January 11, 1982

Q: Why would you throw a lemon down the garbage disposal?
Paul: Because it was very, very naughty.

Paul was a Heatter/Quigley regular. He'd been on *The Celebrity Game, Funny You Should Ask,* and *P.D.Q.* He showed up now and then on *The Hollywood Squares,* but he didn't become a regular until the fall of 1968. Les Roberts was producing the show then and it was a double-taping, meaning we taped for two days in a row. Jackie Mason had been in the center square on Saturday and was booked to do the show again on Sunday. As Les was leaving the studio late that night, he saw Jackie Mason getting into his car. "See you tomorrow," he said.

"I don't think so," said Jackie.

"What do you mean?" Les began to panic. After all, it was midnight on Saturday and if Mason backed out, he'd be missing one star the next day.

"To tell you the truth," said Jackie, "I'm too big for this show."

Les immediately drove back to the office and called Mary Markham and Gary Damsker and told them he had to have a star for the center square by tomorrow morning. After going through all the people who couldn't make it, Gary finally told Les he could try London Lee, Charlie Callas, or Paul Lynde. Because Paul had done so many Heatter/Quigley shows and was playing Uncle Arthur on *Bewitched* at the time, Les chose Paul. This turned out to be a very good choice, and when I got to the studio the next day, I was happy. Jackie Mason was always my least favorite square.

Paul became the most popular star on the show and the only panelist to be honored with two daytime Emmy Awards—one in 1975 and one in 1979, both for Outstanding Individual Achievement in Daytime Programming.

It kind of makes me laugh, because Paul's persona would be so politically incorrect today that he'd probably never be allowed on network television, let alone be given an award for it. One of the jokes that was in particularly bad taste comes to mind. The question was, "You've got a brown rug, brown walls, brown furniture, brown appliances. What does that indicate?" Paul's joke: "The maid exploded."

Of course, Paul didn't write this joke. Harry Friedman did and it was one of his shining moments on the show. Mel Brooks called the next day to say it was the funniest thing he'd seen on television in a long time. But Harry wrote it for Paul's personality and that was what made our show great. If Paul had had the talent or inclination to write his own jokes, they would have been exactly what our writers wrote for him—only probably not as good.

And then there was his attitude. That kind of snarling, angry bitchiness that made him everybody's favorite was really not a put-on at all. Paul was a pretty unhappy guy with a lot of neuroses and not too many things in his life that he loved. He was crazy about his dog, a Dandie Dinmont terrier he named Harry MacAfee after his character in *Bye Bye, Birdie*. Harry really was Paul's best friend and Paul enjoyed spoiling him rotten. He even went so far as to send Harry to Kansas City when it was time to get groomed. Paul couldn't find a dog groomer in all of Southern California who was good enough to bathe and snip his pooch.

Paul got more mail than anyone on the show—almost exclusively from women.

Whenever The Lennon Sisters did our show, we put them on both sides of the center square, two in each box, and Paul was in heaven. He absolutely adored them and it was fun for me to watch Paul on his best behavior. Of course, his favorite was always Karen Valentine. They had met a few years before, on the set of *Gidget Grows Up*, and they became very close after Karen started doing *Squares* regularly. To this day, I harbor a belief that it broke Paul's heart that the two of them could only be friends. He related to her in a way I never saw him do with another woman.

He also loved good food and, of course, booze (or as he called it,

Paul usually brought Harry MacAfee to the studio,
but we seldom put him on the show. Paul was expensive enough.

"boooooze"). One night at dinner, Paul got so drunk I don't even know how we got through the last two shows. After the taping, I begged him to let me drive him home, but he insisted he was perfectly fine. I could see he wasn't, and there wasn't enough money in the world to keep him out of jail if he got another DUI, but there didn't seem to be anything I could do about it.

We were double-taping that week, so it was a big relief for me to see Paul come strolling into the studio the next day. Then I heard the story. He was driving home, on the sidewalk, when a cop pulled him over. The cop walked over to the car, opened his book, and took out his pencil, and Paul said, "I'll have a cheeseburger, hold the fries." Luckily the cop was a *Squares* fan. He said, "All right, Mr. Lynde. Let's go home now." So instead of a ticket, Paul got a police escort to his house.

That wasn't the only time Paul got out of a serious scrape because of his popularity. In the summer of 1974, while touring in his home state of Ohio with the Kenley Players, he pulled a prank that could have given anyone else some heavy-duty problems. He got arrested for yelling obscenities at a patrol officer. Charged with public intoxication, Paul showed up in a Toledo courtroom that was filled to capacity. The judge allowed forty people to stand after all the seats were taken. It was a pretty big shock to Paul when he was found guilty, but I think the punishment ordered by the judge kind of made up for the verdict. The fine was $100 and $10 in court costs, and this little sojourn on the other side of the law never seemed to hurt his popularity. Turns out his fans were more disappointed because he wouldn't sign autographs after his trial than they were by his questionable moral antics.

In 1976, Paul was touring in his own show. He discovered Wayland Flowers & Madame in a Florida bar. At the time, Wayland was a struggling ventriloquist, and when he would run out of money for drinks, he'd bring his dummy, Madame, out of a violin case. She was irresistibly funny, and people would buy her drinks, which Wayland would enjoy. They became one of Paul's opening acts and later became semi-regulars on *Squares*.

We had to be careful who we put next to Paul, because if he was seated next to someone he didn't like, he became insufferable, and if he ever took a dislike to a contestant, that guy might as well have gone home. He'd do everything he could to make that person lose. He'd practically come right out and say his answer was correct and force the contestant to agree. Of course, his answer would be wrong. Then, during the commercial, he'd say, "Got you, didn't I?" I'd tell the poor contestant to ignore him, but that was pretty hard to do when Paul was being evil.

But he sure could make me laugh. I'll never forget the time he had to use the dressing room the *Gold Diggers* had been in that afternoon. He walked in, wrinkled up his nose, and said, "This room smells like pussy. Of course, that's just a guess on my part."

When Paul quit the show, *The National Enquirer* reported that he was forced out because of "drinking and other nastiness," and Paul sued them for $10 million. The truth was, Paul left because he wanted more money. And he didn't come back to the show until he got it.

Early in 1982, Paul agreed to do a pilot that Jay Redack was producing. It involved shooting at Paul's home, and Jay arrived there on the appointed day with full camera crew, ready to go to work. He rang the doorbell and pounded on the door. No answer. He noticed the Sunday paper was still in the driveway and heard Paul's dog, Harry, barking his head off in the house, but Paul didn't come to the door. Jay figured he'd spent the night out and not even bothered to come home to keep the appointment and he was pretty upset. He left Paul a note that said something like, "Paul, Goddammit, this meant a lot to me and you really screwed me up. Here's the number where we'll be next. Call me as soon as you get in. This is really important." At the next shoot, Jay got a call from the police. They said they needed to talk to him. Paul Lynde had been found in his home, dead.

Paul was once on the cover of *People* magazine and was quoted as saying, "My following is straight. I'm so glad. Y'know gay people killed Judy Garland, but they're not going to kill me." I never could figure out what he meant by that, but I loved something I read about him in *Out* magazine. They described him as Paul Lynde, the gay icon who made the world a safer place for sissies.

6

X Gets the Square

George Gobel, Vincent Price, Mel Brooks, and many
of the other male stars we came to love on the show.

George Gobel
May 20, 1919–February 24, 1991

> *Q:* True or false? A pea can last as long as five thousand years.
> *George:* Boy, sometimes it sure seems like it

People always ask me who was my all-time favorite Hollywood Square.
Without a moment's hesitation, I can answer that question: George Gobel.
He was also my closest friend on the show. It took me two years of constant
badgering to get him there, but I never let him know what I was trying to
do. Finally, when Cliff started to get so sick that we feared (and rightly so)

Here's George with
Bob at a party at
Merrill's house.

he wouldn't be able to do the show much longer, Merrill and Bob agreed to give George a try.

I remember how excited I was. I went right down to The Tail Of The Cock on Ventura where I knew I'd find George at the bar. "Hey, you're going to do *Squares*," I said.

He looked at me for a long moment before he said, "Why would I want to do that?"

Now I knew George was actually afraid to go on the show. He didn't think he could be funny anymore, which was ludicrous. So I handled it in my own tactful manner.

"Shut up," I explained. "You're doing the damned show."

So he did, and the rest was *Hollywood Squares* history. His quiet, laid-back style was perfect for the show and when Cliffie died in 1972, George became a regular, taking over the lower right square.

As with so many fine performers, George had been a child entertainer. As a youngster he made frequent appearances on the *National Barn Dance* and played all the kid parts on the *Tom Mix* radio show. Like mine, George's career was interrupted by World War II. He served as a flight instructor in the Army Air Corps. After his stint in the service, most of which he spent safely in Tulsa, Oklahoma, he went back to performing. He did stand-up comedy in nightclubs and in 1954 he got his own show on CBS, *The George Gobel Show*. It lasted until 1960, and George was hot.

During the heyday of *The Hollywood Squares*, I was invited to perform constantly. I loved working clubs with The Chapter Five, but I think the most fun I had was playing venues like *Knott's Berry Farm* with George. I couldn't believe the college-age audiences that would turn out to see him and give him standing ovations, and he was funny. It always amazed me to watch from the wings as an aging George would get out there and become Lonesome George from the fifties. When he said his famous line, "Well, I'll be a dirty bird," the audience would just go nuts. At the end of his act, the kids would scream for an encore. They couldn't get enough of him.

George used to appear on *The Tonight Show* quite regularly. He would have his regular interview, and then Johnny would ask him if anything of note had happened on *The Hollywood Squares* lately. George would pull out some index cards and read some questions and answers and get screams. Here is one that typified George to me.

Q: If you find someone lying unconscious in the street, should you do anything?

George: I'd probably crawl around him, I guess.

I remember working at Lake Tahoe with George. One night, the phone rang in my room at about three in the morning. It was Greg Gobel, George's

Opposite page: George drinking coffee on the set—or is that coffee?

son. Seemed his dad was at the blackjack table having a wonderful time and refusing to come upstairs. Sally had a real way with George, so she got dressed and went down to the casino and sure enough, there was George with a tall drink and a big pile of chips in front of him. Sally walked up behind him.

"Hey, sailor," she said. "What do you say we go up to your room?" George puffed up like a peacock as heads turned his way. With a big smile, he gathered up his chips and 5 foot 1 inch George and 5 foot 9 inch Sally walked away from the table. As they approached the elevators, George turned to the casino and took a big bow, and the people he'd been playing blackjack with applauded.

George loved to drink and he loved to play golf, and one day he had a date to play Lakeside, an exclusive country club in Toluca Lake, California, that was always full of local and visiting celebrities. After the game, George went to the locker room and there was President Nixon. They were introduced, Nixon invited him to have a drink and, of course, George accepted. Now some of you may remember George talking about spooky old Alice on his television show. Well, his wife was a little different from Phyllis Diller's husband, Fang. She really was spooky old Alice, not just somebody a comedian created to get laughs, although she did serve that purpose quite well. In fact, I don't remember any of her friends ever calling her Alice—to us she was always Spooky. Anyway, Spooky called the country club looking for George, and the bartender put him on the phone.

"Where the hell are you?" she shrilled.

"I'm sitting here having a drink with the president of the United States."

"Bullshit," answered Spooky.

With that, George handed the phone to Nixon. "Hello, Alice," he said. I guess he didn't feel comfortable calling her Spooky. "This is Richard Nixon. So nice to speak with you."

"Whoever you are," said Spooky, "you're full of shit. Now send that little fucker home."

Buddy Hackett

Buddy did the show quite frequently in the beginning, and he was a bright and funny guest. He was also the most intolerant man I've ever met. In those days, lots of people smoked, but not if Buddy was around—unless you enjoyed being harangued within an inch of your life. One night, Zsa Zsa brought her little dog in to the dinner hall. Buddy entered wearing the bright yellow terrycloth robe he always donned between shows, and immediately started yelling at her for bringing an animal in where people were eating. An embarrassed hush fell over the room and I was just getting ready to leap to Zsa Zsa's defense, when she pointed a long, painted fingernail at him. "Get out of here, you little yellow lemon," she ordered.

Buddy very seldom missed an answer, for two good reasons. First, he's an intelligent, well-read man. Second, once he knew the areas of the questions he was going to be asked, he would actually study up for the show. Compliance and Practices got suspicious about Buddy always being right and came into the room with the producer when he was being briefed to make sure no one was giving him the answers. That night I asked Buddy a medical question and his answer didn't match the one I had on the card. I said, "Looks like you finally missed one, Buddy." Well, Buddy got upset and during the break went out to his car and got a medical book he'd been reading, and there was the answer he'd given—the correct one. Of course, we brought the contestant back, so there was no harm done. At least, not that time.

Buddy was on our show often, but when he started doing another game show at NBC called *Celebrity Sweepstakes*, Merrill and Bob stopped using him. I guess Buddy's feelings must have been hurt by that, because he went on *The Tonight Show* and told the world that the reason *Sweepstakes* was different from *Squares* was that on *Celebrity Sweepstakes* the stars weren't given the answers. Well, we didn't give stars the answers, at least not as a general practice, and even if we had it would have had no effect on the outcome of the game, so it seemed that Buddy had done a pretty mean-spirited thing. Our show came under investigation and came very close to being taken off the air. To protect the show, Merrill and Bob agreed to run a disclaimer at the close. This is what they came up with:

> The areas of questions designed for each celebrity and possible bluff answers are discussed with each celebrity in advance. In the course of their briefing, actual questions and answers may be given or discerned by the celebrities.

Of course, they ran it so fast, it was completely indecipherable.

I interviewed Mike Landon for an upcoming NBC Show.

Michael Landon

October 31, 1936—July 1, 1991

Mike was one of the cutest guys I've ever known, a caring, serious-minded filmmaker with a conscience—and the primary reason I had to give up tomato soup. Mike told me he once had a summer job at a very well-known soup factory. A very large rat fell into the vat of tomato soup, and Mike had to put on a pair of big plastic wading boots, walk into the vat of soup, and pull the rodent out. After the varmint was disposed of, the production continued as if nothing had happened. All that tomato soup went into cans, into stores, and into people's homes. Now, Mike might have been exaggerating, as so many of us are prone to do when we have a good story to tell—and even if it *were* true, that was a long time ago and I'm sure sanitary conditions have improved tremendously since then. But I have a pretty queasy stomach and no matter how much I miss my tomato soup, I just haven't been able to bring myself to eat it, ever again.

Mike's mother was Peggy O'Neill before she married his father, Eli Orowitz, and was so beautiful that a song was written about her. It was called *Sweet Peggy O'Neill* and was a monster hit of the time. In her later years, she truly proceeded to drive Mike crazy, but he was always a wonderful son. I remember times when he was on the set and we'd get an emergency call. Mike's mother had her head in the oven and wasn't going to take it out until he came to the phone. Needless to say, Mike would always manage to get to the phone and deal with it.

He once told me the most important thing his mother taught him was how to run. Some of you might be familiar with Mike's problem as a bedwetter. He did a very big after-school special about it. He said when he was a kid, he had to run home as fast as he could because his mother would hang

Two Mikes and a Mary: Mike Landon, Mike Connors, and Mary Markham sharing a laugh at dinner.

his wet sheets out the upstairs window and if the other kids got there before he did, they would see them and know what he had done.

I remember Mike as a great bluffer on the show, but more than that I remember the sweet things he did. He was on the first show we taped after Wally died, and he was sitting in Wally's box next to Rose Marie. At one point, Ro looked over, saw Mike instead of Wally and choked up. At the break, he came up to her and put his arms around her. "It's okay, honey," he said. "He's still here. He's watching us." Ro said it made her feel better, and she's never forgotten it.

Then there was the night Mike came to a taping and I could tell he'd been drinking, which was very unusual for Mike. Turns out he had come directly from the taping of *Bonanza*, and during that taping, the network pulled the plug on the show—no warning, nothing. Mike had had the same production staff and crew for the length of the show, and he was upset because all of those people were now out of work. Never a word about himself.

Rodney Dangerfield

Rodney was very nervous about doing the show, because he wasn't sure how to work his jokes in and didn't know if he would get questions that would work for his material. He was in Vegas at the time and didn't want to wait until tape day to get briefed, so Jay agreed to do it over the phone. Jay called Rodney at his hotel and explained that the briefing was just to give him some idea of the area of questions that would be asked so he could be prepared with possible bluffs or jokes, then told him to get a paper and pencil. "Now write this down," said Jay. "The first question is about men's shorts. Have you got it?"

"I'm writing it down," said Rodney. "Men's shorts."

"The next question is about something that young boys do, are you writing it down?"

"I'm writing it down," said Rodney. "What young boys do."

"The next question—"

"Hold it," said Rodney. "I'm not going to do this anymore."

"Why not?" asked Jay.

"Because the maid's starting to look at me funny and I think I'm going to be arrested."

And that was the end of that briefing.

Rich Little

On Mother's Day, 1976, Rich Little saved the show. Our associate producer, Harry Friedman, had taken his wife, Judy, out to brunch to celebrate her first year as a mom, and from there he was heading straight to the studio for an afternoon taping. Their brunch was interrupted by an emergency call from Gary Damsker. Two of our stars had dropped out and because of the holiday, Gary couldn't find anybody to replace them.

This was a problem we'd never faced before, and a serious one. With two stars missing, it looked like the taping would have to be canceled and that

John Davidson enjoyed showing Rich Little that he could do impersonations, too. He didn't have a clue that the guy he was impersonating was standing right behind him.

would have cost a ton of money. All the stars who were booked would have to be paid as well as the technicians, caterers, hair, and makeup, and we'd have no shows. Harry made the decision to stay cool, go to the studio, and hope that one of our Toluca Lake regulars—JoAnne Worley, Robert Fuller, or Dick Patterson—would be reachable by the time he got there, or that one of the folks Gary had calls out to would have responded. There was also always the chance someone else would be taping and we could snag a star who had finished on a different show.

But, alas, it was Mother's Day and no one was available from any of those sources. Harry was about to give up when he realized that one of the stars booked that day was Rich Little, and you could almost see the light bulb go off over his head. He went into a huddle with Rich and I saw Rich smiling and nodding his head. Next thing I knew, Rich was in the top center square flanked by—nobody. Whenever a contestant had to go to one of the top corners, Rich would move into that square and answer the question as whoever the question prompted him to be.

After the show, I congratulated Rich on the brilliant job he did, and he said the weirdest part about the whole thing was when he had to return to the middle square and answer questions as himself.

Dick Patterson

Dick Patterson was not a *Hollywood Squares* semi-regular—he was more of a Heatter/Quigley semi-regular. For years, Dick appeared on H-Q game shows such as *P.D.Q.* and did run-throughs for them when they wanted to try out a new show, but perhaps he made himself too available. He seemed to fall into that category of people who you never thought to book on his own, but let someone not show up, and Dick, who lived only minutes away from NBC, was delighted to take that person's place. I felt it was unkind, in a way, but Dick didn't seem to mind. He was always up and happy to get the gig, and he did a very nice job on the show.

One time Wally didn't arrive for a taping and no one could reach him by phone. It was getting closer and closer to tape time and still no Wally. *Laugh-In* wasn't taping that night and there was no one on the *Tonight Show* we could grab, so we called Dick. Luckily, or so we all thought at the time, he was home and available. He rushed right over to the studio, the technicians changed the name on the box from Wally Cox to Dick Patterson, and Dick climbed the stairs to the top right box just as I started the warm-up. Now, Dick came prepared. He had a little window shade that he could pull up and down, a Groucho nose and glasses, and the ever-popular rubber chicken. Installed in his square, Dick couldn't have been happier.

Suddenly, through the doors of the studio burst Wally—his face was lit up, he was just beaming. He apologized for being late and explained that he was riding his motorcycle to work and he spotted a rare butterfly and started to chase it. He didn't want to catch it, just look at it, which was what he did. And he was there in time to put on his rumpled brown suit and get to his box before the taping began.

The problem became what to do with Dick Patterson. Nobody wanted to be the one to tell him he wasn't going to do the show after all. I sure wasn't going to do it. Finally, our producer, Jay Redack, got unanimously elected. As the technicians were changing the name on the box back to Wally Cox, Jay climbed the stairs that led to the top row of the set and whispered to Dick. Dick kind of smiled—he was so sweet about it—packed up his props, and walked down the stairs, careful not to look out at the audience. It was one of the worst moments I can remember from the show. And Jay told me recently that if there was one thing he could undo in all the years he was with the show, that would have been it.

Burt Reynolds

When Burt started doing *The Hollywood Squares* in the late sixties, his television series, *Dan August,* had fizzled and his career was in somewhat of a slump. He and Bill Armstrong were quite friendly at the time, and Bill talked Merrill into putting Burt on *Squares.*

Burt actually credits that first appearance with saving his career. Someone from *The Tonight Show* happened to catch him on *Squares* and he was so cute and funny they decided to book him. A film producer saw him on *The Tonight Show* and that led to his being cast in the movie *Deliverance.* Then he did the nude *Cosmopolitan* magazine layout, and the rest is show biz history.

Burt became a very big star, but he never forgot his friends. I think Burt will go farther for a friend than almost anyone I know. He used to fly in from Florida to do *Squares* during sweeps week, and later, when Bill was emceeing a syndicated game show called *Liar's Club*, Burt agreed to appear on the show although he had invested in a fighter who was fighting for the very first time that night.

And because Norman Fell, another good friend of Burt's, hadn't been working very much, Burt asked Bill to book him on *Liar's Club*, too. Of course, Bill did, making it possible for Good Buddy Burt to accomplish two acts of friendship in one night.

Dale Robertson

Dale and I have been friends for many years. We were in drama school together in Hollywood along with a wonderful actress by the name of Rhoda Jacobs, who later changed her name to Piper Laurie. Dale was this gorgeous guy who made $150 a week at Fox and drove a big old beat-up Cadillac convertible. He was so good-looking that he did a walk-on in a movie and got more fan mail than Tyrone Power. That's when Fox decided to make him a star.

In those days, you knew you had made it when Louella Parsons asked you to be on her show. Well, she called Dale's agent and invited Dale on, and of course the agent said yes, but before he could tell his client about it, Dale ran into Louella at a Hollywood hot spot.

"I'm so glad you're going to be on my show," she said.

Dale was a little taken aback, but he recovered quickly. "I'm looking forward to it," he said. "By the way, how much do you pay?"

"Pay!" gasped Louella. Apparently this Okie didn't know that people would have gladly paid her to be on her show.

"You don't do the show for free," said Dale. "Why should I?"

"You're going to be out of this business in a year," declared Louella, then turned and marched away.

A couple of days later, when Dale was sitting in Harry Cohn's office at Columbia Pictures, the phone rang. It was Louella Parsons calling Harry to tell him not to hire an arrogant young actor named Dale Robertson. "Not only is he arrogant," she went on, "but I believe he's anti-Semitic.

After Louella hung up, Cohn asked Dale if he was anti-Semitic.

Dale thought about this, then said, "What's that mean?"

"That you don't like Jews."

"Oh," said Dale. "Are you a Jew?"

Cohn replied, "I certainly am."

"Well, I sure don't like you!" Their friendship continued until Harry's death, and Dale went on to make 63 motion pictures and 430 hours of television.

My friendship with Dale has never faltered. His mother and my mother were very close, both active in the Motion Picture Moms, and his first wife and my sister were best friends. Dale was born in Oklahoma, and that's where he lives today with his wife, Susan, and a bunch of horses, dogs, cats, and peacocks. We still see a lot of each other at celebrity golf tournaments.

Vincent Price
May 27, 1911–October 25, 1993

Q: One of the most famous paintings by the French artist Renoir is called Two Girls at—at what?

Vincent: At once.

When I was seventeen, I loved going to Fox studios where my brother-in-law, Dick Haymes, was a huge star. What kid wouldn't love that, you're probably thinking. The glamour, the action, the excitement. Well, that wasn't exactly it—it was because I had a huge crush on the 1940s film star

He looked like he took the game seriously, but Vinnie was really a very funny guy.

June Haver, who later married my good friend Fred MacMurray, and that was the only way I got to see her. But while I was there, I did get to meet people such as Vincent Price. Unlike his public persona, Vincent was the sweetest, most gentle man you'd ever want to meet. Through the years, I saw Vincent occasionally, but I was always in awe of him until he started doing *Squares*. That's when I found out he knew absolutely nothing about Shakespeare, and he became a little more accessible to me. We became close friends.

He and his second wife, Mary, would travel the world collecting recipes from all the great restaurants. In 1965, they published the most gorgeous cookbook I've ever owned, *A Treasury of Great Recipes*. I'd put his wilted spinach salad up against anybody's.

While Vinnie was married to Mary, something quite unexpected happened. He was filming the great 1973 comedy classic *Theater of Blood*. If you're a fan of Vincent's, or even of the horror/comedy genre, and you've never seen *Theater of Blood*—what are you waiting for? The best scene in the movie has Vinnie posing as a hair stylist with an afro before disposing of his client, one of the uppity critics who had blasted his work as an actor a year earlier.

At the age of sixty-two, Vinnie fell head over heels in love with the woman who played that unfortunate critic in the film, the superb Australian actress Coral Browne. Coral, at fifty-nine, also found the love of her life in him. It must have been difficult for Vinnie to tell Mary he wanted a divorce after twenty-three years of marriage, but the love he and Coral shared was a once-in-a-lifetime thing that couldn't be denied. He adored Coral until her death from cancer in 1991. Vincent Price died two short years later.

My second wife, Sally, and I accompanied Vincent and Coral on their honeymoon cruise. One passenger on the ship, a rather rude American woman, wouldn't leave Vincent alone. He and Coral would be playing backgammon or trying to enjoy a drink on the deck, and this woman would start talking to them. Vincent was the kindest man alive, so he would always be polite and Coral, who appeared to be a very grand and proper Englishwoman, put up with the woman's pushy behavior as long as she could. Imagine the woman's surprise when Coral finally turned to her, smiled sweetly, and said, "Dahling, would you do us a favor and please fuck off?" That was Coral.

On the first morning, Sally went down to meet Vincent and Coral a little ahead of me. "Well, you two lovebirds," she said, "did you have a good night?"

"As a matter of fact, dahling," said Coral, "we were talking about you."

"Me?" said Sally. "I'd think you'd have better things to talk about on your wedding night than me."

Vincent smiled and chucked her under the chin. "We were just saying what a nice little tidbit you'd make for Coral and me." Vinnie was always full of surprises.

Like the time he and Coral bought a motor home. It was always kind of hard for me to imagine Mr. and Mrs. Price driving around the country in an RV, but that's exactly what they did. One night, he got delayed while heading home for a taping. By the time he got there, he'd driven way too many miles and had way too much to drink. He got to the taping exhausted, his head pounding with a massive hangover. When I introduced the guests to the studio audience, I always intro'd Vinnie as "the boogie man himself" and out came Vinnie, who never complained about anything, to take his

Bob Quigley, Coral Browne, Vincent Price, and Elaine Healler.

83

bow. Now the audience is yelling and screaming, and Vinnie is bowing and smiling, and under his breath he's saying, "Shut up, shut up."

As I said, Vincent was a kind and gentle man, but he was excruciatingly honest. Once he was on the show with Rich Little, who proudly did his impersonation of Vincent. Vinnie cringed. "That's the worst me I ever heard!" he said.

Another time, Vincent and I were walking to the parking lot when a woman stopped us and asked for our autographs. I signed my name. Then it was Vinnie's turn. "Dolores Del Rio," he wrote with a flourish. The woman left happily, never glancing at her autographs.

"Vinnie," I said, "I'm not sure that was very nice. That woman's going to be very unhappy when she gets home and finds she has an autograph of a silent film actress instead of yours."

Vinnie just smiled. "Before she died, Dolores said to me, 'Don't *ever* let them forget me,' so now I always sign Dolores Del Rio."

If it weren't so presumptuous, I'd start signing my autograph "Vincent Price."

7

Circle Gets the Square

We can't forget Rose Marie, Nanette Fabray, Abby Dalton, and the rest of the women who made the show so much fun to watch.

Rose Marie

> Q: During a tornado, are you safer in the bedroom or in the closet?
> Rose Marie: Unfortunately I'm always safe in the bedroom.

Ro was cast on our show as the woman who couldn't get a man, like her character, Sally, on *The Dick Van Dyke Show*. In truth, Rose Marie was happily married for many years to the love of her life, the great trumpet player Bobby Guy. When he died unexpectedly after a sudden illness, Ro suddenly felt like she couldn't do anything anymore. She couldn't sing, she couldn't dance. She certainly couldn't handle another show like *Dick Van Dyke*. Mary Markham convinced her to do the game show for a while. Mary said it would be good for her—it would help get her back in the groove and she wouldn't have to sing, dance, or act. And Mary was right. Ro did *Squares* from beginning to end and became the woman most associated with the show.

Rose Marie was no stranger to show business. As "Baby Rose Marie" she was knockin' 'em dead before most kids her age had started kindergarten. You've got to picture this little girl on stage, playing to a packed house as she belted out a number like she was Ethel Merman. She starred in the short made to accompany the premiere of *The Jazz Singer* at the Wintergarten Theater in New York in 1929, a huge theatrical event. The tiny trooper finished her number and was handed two bouquets of roses that were almost as big as she was. The audience was demanding an encore and Ro, a born professional, thrust the flowers at the stage manager and said, "Hold the roses. I can't take my bow."

Rose Marie was as much a part of the show as the NBC peacock.

Since then, Ro's done everything from performing for the mob in Vegas to working on behalf of muscular dystrophy in Canada. And, of course, she's entertained us with countless hours of television and film performances. Probably the one she's best known for, not counting *Squares*, was her role as Sally on *The Dick Van Dyke Show*. Ro told me she auditioned for that part for years. She kept nagging Sheldon Leonard to put her on *The Danny Thomas Show*. Finally, he called her into the office. When she got there, she found out they wanted her for a role on a brand new show, *The Dick Van Dyke Show*. Ro was a little disappointed, but she always loved to work, so she took the part.

Before the show's premiere, she was asked to travel to radio stations across the country to do promos. Now, let me tell you something. I've done radio promo tours and it's about as much fun as getting pecked to death by ducks. You're up at the crack of dawn, you spend most of your time in cars, airports, and radio stations, and you usually do something like twenty-five cities in eighteen days, so you really don't get to see anything or anybody. But Rose Marie is a real team player, so off she went and when she got to Cleveland, something happened that made it all worthwhile. She discovered Tim Conway.

There she was, giving her spiel for the show, when a disembodied voice began to interrupt her. She'd start over, and the voice would interrupt her again. It was kind of irritating, but the guy was really funny. When she finally finished the spots, she asked to meet the clown who was giving her all the trouble. Out came a young disc jockey who apologized for any inconvenience. But Rose Marie didn't want to chastise him—she wanted to know if he had a tape she could bring back to Hollywood.

She played that tape for her husband and he said, "Sign him." Ro protested that she wasn't a manager, but Bobby insisted, so Ro got Tim Conway to sign a contract with her as his manager. Actually, it was Tom Conway at the time, but because there was already an actor by that name, they changed his name to Tim. Upon her return to Hollywood, Rose Marie took the tape to Steve Allen, who decided to use Tim on his new show. Ro got Tim round-trip airfare from Cleveland (in case he had to go back) and $1,000, and that was the beginning of a very big career.

Besides discovering Tim Conway, Ro was famous for the sumptuous dinners we shared at her home. She was the ultimate Italian mama to us all, spreading her table with pasta, sausage, eggplant, and every delicacy you can imagine, and urging us to eat until we were ready to pop. One night she had dinner scheduled at seven. At six she was in her bathrobe combing her hair when the doorbell rang. It was Vincent Price carrying a carton of red and white wine.

"Vincent, what are you doing here an hour early?" she asked. "I'm not even ready yet."

He brushed right past her and into the kitchen, opened two bottles of wine and headed back for the front door. "I wanted to be sure the wine had the proper amount of time to breathe," said the consummate gourmet. Who then left and came back at seven.

Nanette Fabray

Q: When wearing a kilt, where does a Scotsman keep his dirk?
Nanette: Tucked in the top of his stocking.

If you had agreed, you would have gotten the square, but the rest of the panel was laughing so hard at the question, poor Nanette could barely make her equally funny answer. We liked to give Nanette these kinds of questions for two reasons. One, she was Scottish by marriage—her husband was Randall MacDougall, one of the top ten screenwriters of the day—and two, she had a "nice" persona that made it fun to see her respond to double-entendre questions like this.

In reality, Nanette was a funny, rowdy lady. She used to order her martinis with no ice because she was convinced she got more booze that way. I'll never forget the first time I went to her home and saw the needlepoint sampler she had done hanging over her bed. It had little flowers and birds inside an old-fashioned wooden frame, and in the middle the legend "It Takes a Heap of Humping to Make a House a Home."

After much success on Broadway and in movies, she moved into television as one of the stars of *Caesar's Hour.* That show earned her three Emmys and a week in the hospital.

The show was done live, and during one show, a pipe fell and hit her on the head. She was carried out of the studio unconscious, and both the home and studio audience thought she had been killed. Sid Caesar, always the complete professional, finished the show, not knowing if his costar was dead or alive. Luckily for all of us, Nanette was okay, but she was hospitalized for a week. Poor Sid, who was deathly afraid of hospitals, had to go there to film a segment for the next week's show to prove to the world that Nanette was still with us.

There was another side to Nanette that we saw the first time Burt Reynolds did the show. He was in the square next to hers and through the five shows he flirted with her outrageously. Nanette and Ran were newly married and she loved him madly, yet she couldn't help but be aware of Burt's animal magnetism. She said he made her feel all fluttery and sexy. So

From the **TV** movie, *Happy Anniversary and Goodbye,* starring **Art Carney,** whom I adored, **Nanette Fabray,** whom I adored, and **Lucille Ball.**

for five shows Nanette blushed and giggled and had a really good time. Then she went home to her husband and said, "Ran, I absolutely adore you but, oh, that Burt Reynolds."

Nanette's closest friend on the show was Wally Cox. Wally loved his motorcycle and almost always rode it to work, but sometimes his chemical imbalance kicked in and he became absolutely phobic about his bike. When that happened, he'd call Nanette and ask if she would pick him up and, of course, she always did.

Those of you who used to watch the show might remember a funny little wave that Nanette did when Kenny Williams introduced her. She would hold up her thumb, her first finger, and her pinky. That was the first time sign language was used on television and many hearing-impaired people would tune in just to see Nanette signing "I love you." Nan learned to sign because she had been told she was going deaf. Four surgeries corrected the problem, but she's worked hard on behalf of the deaf population and other handicapped people ever since, receiving countless awards over the years for public service. The one I remember most was from the American Academy of Otolaryngology. It had been presented to her just before she came to a taping, and this was only the second time this award had ever been given. Its other recipient? Helen Keller.

Abby Dalton

Abby started her career as one of the Copa girls at the Sands Hotel in Las Vegas. From there, she modeled in New York, was a dancer at the Moulin Rouge in Hollywood, studied acting with Jeff Corey, and starred in four Roger Corman movies. Then she started doing television. First *Hennesey*, then *The Joey Bishop Show*, and that's what eventually brought her to *The Hollywood Squares*.

Allen Ludden had invited Joey Bishop to be on *Password* and he agreed to do it, but only if the other star was Abby. You see, in his mind, Abby was a dumb blonde who had never done a game show before. You see, Joey didn't like to lose, and he was sure he could win all the games against her. Boy, was he wrong! Abby figured out how the game was played in no time and thoroughly enjoyed trouncing the competitive Mr. Bishop. She was so good that Allen Ludden invited her to come back. Soon she was doing tons of game shows. Abby enjoyed them, as did a lot of celebs, because it gave her a chance to show the audience another side of her, the real Abby Dalton, not just a character someone had invented for her to play on a TV show.

Not only did Abby do lots of game shows, but she also did so many successful pilots that she got nicknamed "the good-luck piece." One of those was the Bert Parks pilot for *The Hollywood Squares*. After the show sold, she was on every single episode the first year; the second year, she alternated

Wally, Abby, Cliff, and me either promoting the show or calling home for money.

with Rose Marie, each doing every other show. By the third year, we were getting so many big names that we started using Abby on a need-and-availability basis.

We never gave jokes to Abby. When we'd try to do that, they would just get in her way, because Abby had an attitude—and that's what made her so great on the show.

With game shows becoming a staple of daytime television, they began sprouting up everywhere and certain celebrities could be seen on more than one show. There was, however, a certain etiquette attached to playing the field and it was important for the stars to observe this. Rose Marie, for example, was invited to do many other shows, but always turned them down out of loyalty to Merrill and Bob. Abby missed a lot of *Hollywood Squares* tapings because she ignored this unwritten rule.

In the beginning, when Abby did the show regularly, she always used to give me a lot of trouble about my pronunciation or my grammar. I'd read a question, and Abby would get that schoolteacherish look and say something like, "Peter, shame on you. You split an infinitive." I'd look around innocently and say, "That wasn't me." As the straight man, I seldom had an opportunity to get a laugh, so I always enjoyed those rare moments and really looked forward to the shows with Abby.

Suddenly, Abby wasn't there anymore. I quickly found out why. Merrill and Bob had another game show called *Name Droppers* that featured three celebrities and a person who in some way had a connection to one of the stars. Contestants had to match star to name dropper. Abby had been prepped to do the show and her name dropper was her husband, Jack Smith.

Before her scheduled appearance on *Name Droppers*, Abby appeared on a pilot for game show packager Ralph Andrews. It was called *It Takes Two* and featured celebrities and their spouses answering questions. Abby felt that since it was a pilot and wouldn't be seen on television, it didn't really matter that Jack was on. And it wasn't the first time Jack had appeared on a game show. He was on a show called *I'll Bet* with Abby and got the biggest laugh I ever heard for a civilian. Host Jack Narz asked Abby, "Who built the first airplane?" and Abby had to bet on whether or not her husband would know the answer. Confident Abby bet it all, $500, that Jack would get it right. When he was asked the question, he answered without hesitating. "The

Wright Brothers. Frank and Lloyd." The audience must have laughed for five minutes.

When Merrill and Bob learned of Abby and Jack's appearance on the Ralph Andrews pilot, they canceled her appearance on *Name Droppers*. Maybe it was a competition thing with Ralph, I don't really know, but they also stopped using Abby on *Squares*.

Now, I never had much clout with my producers when it came to who did the show, but I really missed Abby so I went to Merrill and Bob and asked them to bring her back. I don't know if they listened or just got over being mad, but one night I showed up at the studio and, happily for me, there she was. I never had so much fun being put in my place as I did with Abby.

Karen Valentine

Q: Blue, gray, and humpback are all kinds of something. Kinds of what?
Karen: Colors.

It was always our practice to book people off the hot new shows. They usually got a couple of shots and that was the end of it, but Karen Valentine was so cute and funny that she quickly became our resident dingbat and part of *The Hollywood Squares* family.

As a finalist in the Miss Teenage America Contest, Karen was performing a little number she'd worked out in the empty chicken hatchery at her family's farm in Sebastipole, California. You have to keep in mind that the only mirror she had was long and skinny, so all of Karen's moves were up and down, and according to Karen, she looked pretty funny. Luckily, she was doing a comedy pantomime to Eydie Gorme's *Blame it on the Bossa Nova* and you'll never guess who was watching the show, so I'll tell you. None other than Ed Sullivan.

Two weeks later, Karen and her family flew to New York so she could do *The Ed Sullivan Show*. I know this sounds like one of those corny old Broadway plays about small town girl finds success, but I swear, it's the truth.

First, Ed introduced her as ". . . the youngster from Se-bus-*toe*-pull." I had to write that phonetically, the way I used to write on my question cards, so

Karen, trying to say something mean at my roast.

you'll know how he mispronounced Sebastipole. Then Karen did her number and despite her nervousness, she was good enough for Ed to invite her back. Six months later, Karen made her triumphant return—this time she was actually singing "You Can't Get a Man With a Gun." Well, they gave her a big production number; dancers picked her up and twirled her and set her on a bale of hay in the middle of the stage. Karen had never learned how to be picked up, twirled, or set down, and she wasn't a singer. All she knew was what she'd taught herself in the chicken hatchery.

So you've got to picture this kid, sixteen years old, suddenly realizing the whole world would be watching her live. She hadn't a clue as to what she was doing, and even though Harry Belafonte himself assured her she'd be fine and it was normal to be nervous, she was still scared to death. Between the dress rehearsal and the show, Karen wandered onto the empty stage, sat down on the bale of hay, and started to cry. She wished she was back home in her comfy chicken hatchery and wondered why she ever let herself in for this. Then she heard footsteps from the back of the house and looked up to see Barbra Streisand, who was starring in *Funny Girl* at the time, dripping in mink, and walking straight up the aisle toward her. From behind her she heard a voice, not just any voice, but Ed Sullivan's voice. "Barbra!" From Barbra she heard, "Ed!" Barbra rushed up the aisle and onto the stage. Ed rushed downstage and stopped in front of the bale of hay. They met and shared a big hug, not even noticing the little girl sitting just beneath them. Karen looked up, and in her mind's eye she saw herself on stage with Barbra Streisand and Ed Sullivan and that was it. When it was her turn to go on, she did her number without a hitch and that's what she's been doing ever since.

When Karen auditioned for the part on the TV show *Room 222*, she was working in a little bar on Santa Monica Boulevard, selling beer and playing pool with the customers. She was handed a script and knew this part was meant for her. She went into Gene Reynolds's office to read, and when she bent down to pick up the script, her glasses fell off the top of her head. She grabbed for them and knocked her script onto the floor. When she bent over to pick it up, she knocked her purse off the table, and its contents scattered all over the room. Everything was going wrong, so she turned to Gene Reynolds and said, "I can't understand this. I'm usually very chic." He laughed and told her not to change a thing, just read. She did. His final words to her were, "We'll call you. In the meantime, try not to get hit by a bus."

Ruta Lee

Ruta not only did our show many, many times, but also worked on almost all the Heatter/Quigley shows. You may remember her as the beauty that rolled the dice for Alex Trebek on *High Rollers*.

With her beautiful clothes and perfect hair and makeup, Ruta should have been a movie star in the 1930s. Whenever we went on trips together, she would change for breakfast, lunch, and dinner. Her clothes were always

Above: Ruta, looking gorgeous as always.

Below: Cliff Arquette , Rose Marie, John Davidson, George Gobel,
Kent McCord, me (looking like Professor Harold Hill in that jacket),
Vincent Price, Paul Lynde, and in front, Ruta Lee and Sandy Duncan
celebrating our two thousandth show.

elegant, tasteful, and totally appropriate. Ruta was very mindful of looking the part of a movie star when she was in public, because she never wanted to disappoint her fans.

Now I don't mean to make this sound as if Ruta were shallow— anything but. Ruta is of Lithuanian background and became a U.S. citizen at the age of sixteen. From that moment, she began trying to get her grandmother into the United States from Siberia. This was no easy task, as she needed to write an invitation proving she was capable of taking care of her grandmother, that invitation had to be translated into Lithuanian and Russian, and all three invitations had to be notarized and get a city seal and a state seal and be approved by the State Department. Then it had to be sent to her grandmother in Siberia who would take it to the commissar. He would glance at it and say *"Nyet."* Ruta did this every six months to no avail.

One night she came home to find her mother in tears. Her grandmother was dying in a Siberian hospital. Ruta picked up the phone and placed a person to person call to Premier Kruschev himself. Through sheer persistence, she finally got through, explained the situation, and was told to call the Russian Embassy in Washington. Within forty-eight hours, Ruta and her parents were on a plane to Russia. Her grandmother recovered and six months later Ruta returned to Siberia and brought her to the United States. She lived in America for exactly two years, two months, and two days before she died in her mid-nineties.

Jacqueline Susann
August 20, 1921-September 21, 1974

Whenever Jacqueline Susann did the show, she always brought her husband and manager, Irving Mansfield, with her. She didn't know, and he had probably forgotten, that when he was booking *Arthur Godfrey's Talent Scouts* he had turned me down as a singer. Well, I certainly hadn't forgotten. I told him he wasn't allowed on the set and would have to stay in the dressing room during the taping. I let him bumble around a little before I told him I was just kidding and he was welcome on the set. Revenge is sweet.

Jacqueline Susann was so nice, I just couldn't keep her husband, Irving Mansfield, locked in the dressing room, even though he had once turned me down as a singer.

Margaret Truman

Our show was very eclectic in its bookings, and, under normal circumstances, I never knew who was going to be on until I showed up at the studio and saw the set. The first time I saw Margaret Truman's name, I was delighted. Her father, Harry Truman, was always my hero. She had agreed to be on the show for two reasons. One, she had a book to plug, and two, *The Hollywood Squares* was her father's favorite program. She told me President Truman took a walk every morning, and he planned it around our show. If he got up late, he'd watch *Squares*, then take his walk. If he got up early, he'd take his walk, then watch the show.

In 1973, Margaret Truman was on a show with a very special contestant, Lt. David Rehmann, a Navy officer who had spent six years as a POW in Vietnam.

Diana Dors

Diana Dors, who was married to Richard Dawson, only did the show once, but a story was going around that was so funny I never forgot it. She came from a very small village in England and they were so proud of their hometown girl made good, they decided to honor her. It was going to be a lovely ceremony with everyone in town present and the local minister making the opening speech. Diana wasn't born with the glamorous name of Diana Dors; her name was actually Diana Fluck, and the minister was very nervous about possibly mispronouncing the tricky name. He practiced and practiced, and when the time finally came to introduce her he said, "And here she is, the woman we're all so proud of, our very own—Diana Clunt."

I tried to verify this story by asking Les Roberts if it was true. His answer? "God, I hope so."

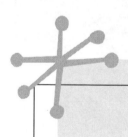

8

Theme Show Squares

Remember the shows built around a theme, like music, sports, and soap operas? Here are the stories.

There came a time when the show started to have a certain sameness about it, and we decided to give it a lift. Somebody, and I don't remember who, came up with what seemed to be a brilliant idea. What if we did some theme shows? You know, one show with all major sports figures, one with all rock and rollers, one with soap opera stars, so we started to drop these theme shows into our schedule.

We did two soap opera shows. Now, I normally wouldn't list every star, but I've heard from some fans that the *TV Guide* listing for those shows was simply "soap opera stars and Paul Lynde," or "sixteen soap stars and Wayland & Madame," so here are the panelists from those shows. If you don't care, just skip over the next paragraph.

In July 1979 we featured Josh Taylor, Val Dufour, Hugh Marlowe and Irene Dailey, Diedre and Andrea Hall, Leslie Dalton and Stephen Yates, Katherine Glass, Tom Licon and Victoria Mallory, Judith McConnell and Dennis Cooney, and Paul Lynde in the center square.

I guess it did all right, because in December 1979, we did it again. This time we had Bill and Susan Seaforth Hayes, Quinn Redeker and Brenda Benet, Richard Guthrie and Tracey Bregman, all from *Days of Our Lives;* with Paul Stevens and Susan Keith from *Another World;* Franc Luz and Nancy Pinkerton from *The Doctors;* Sherry Mathis and Rod Arrants from *Search for Tomorrow;* Brenda Dickson and Bob Colbert from *The Young and the Restless;* Dennis Cooney and Kelly Wood from *As the World Turns;* and Wayland & Madame & Jiffy in the center square.

The sports shows didn't do as well. They were actually the lowest-rated shows we ever did. I guess we should have realized that our viewing audience

Bill and Susan Seaforth Hayes from *Days of Our Lives* were just two of the many soap stars who appeared on our soap opera theme shows.

was mostly women who didn't get turned on by a bunch of athletes, but the guys from the office sure did. They showed up at the studio with their sons, their autograph books, and their cameras.

It wasn't that these athletes were very good at playing the game, and they sure weren't easy to write jokes for. But it was a guy thing and we all just couldn't wait to get our picture taken with Mickey Mantle, Hank Aaron, Bill Walton, or any of the other great athletes who came out to play our game.

And we had music shows. They were always a lot of fun because they were so different from our regular shows. Once again, everybody seemed to want to get in the picture with these stars.

We also did some shows that featured all cast members from a television series or movie. Among them were *Dallas, Eight Is Enough, Silent Movie,* and *Murder by Death*.

One of our players didn't like the theme shows at all. If you guessed Paul, you'd be right on the money. I think he missed all his cronies, since he was the only regular we used. He was also the only one who didn't, and certainly wouldn't, share a square. We were doing a music theme show and everything had moved along so smoothly, we decided to cram in a sixth show at the last minute. Paul was in his dressing room getting ready to leave, and Jay Redack had to go in and tell him he wouldn't be going home quite yet. Paul got so upset he threw Harry MacAfee's dog dish, which was full of kibble at the time, at Jay—then left anyway. It worked out okay, though. KC from KC and the Sunshine Band took over Paul's seat. He might not have been Paul, but he did just fine.

Once in a while, we did a public service program. For example, Seagram's wanted to do a show urging young people to drink sensibly. Jay and Harry went to the Century City Hotel for a lunch meeting with the executives. They walked into a suite and there was every kind of booze known to man. These guys were pouring drinks that would have killed a normal person. Jay and Harry tried to drink sensibly, but it was pretty hard to keep up with the Seagram's guys, so they did the next most sensible thing. They spent the night at the hotel. They did, however, manage to put the deal together.

So one night, after a regular taping, we did this special half-hour show about alcohol abuse that would be shown in public schools. Leslie Uggams and Roddy McDowall were the contestants. I can't remember everyone who was on the panel, but I know Steve Martin called and said he'd received twenty-four cases of liquor from Seagram's in appreciation for doing the show. The writers and producers said trucks would arrive at their homes with barrels filled with boxes of booze. I never even got a bottle.

Mickey Mantle poses with Jay Redack. No wonder all the guys loved the sports shows.

Our three thousandth show featured three Oscar winners: Louise
Fletcher, Marsha Mason, and Eileen Brennan.

We also did a special show to launch a new cereal for Ralston-Purina.
Everybody was raving about all the cereal they received. I didn't get one box.

Laugh-In was never a theme show, but so many of the regulars appeared
on *Squares* at one time or another, I thought of it as sort of a recurring
theme. There was a very good reason for these bookings, besides the fact
that they were brilliant, talented stars with lots of television exposure. It
was that they taped right across the hall from us. Since they never shot in
sequence, somebody was always available for those times when one of our
stars wouldn't show up. We could get them for one show, if someone was
detained, or for all five if we needed them. Many performers from their
show did ours, with three notable exceptions. One, of course, was Dan
Rowan. I would have been very unhappy if anyone had ever booked him
on the show, and I think everybody knew it. I guess that situation would
have made it uncomfortable to book Dick Martin, so we never did. The
third cast member was Goldie Hawn.

I always thought she would have been great on the show. She was so upbeat and cute, with that adorable giggle and the best little body I ever saw. But Goldie had a manager who felt she had big things in store, and a game show appearance wasn't going to help her future plans at all. I guess he was right. Goldie has a fabulous career as a movie star and is probably the most famous alumna of that great show.

Judy Carne did our show often and it was always fun for two reasons. You never knew what she was going to say, and she hardly ever wore panties under the short skirts that were so popular at the time. One night I asked her this question. "In the Bible, Aaron, Moses' brother, had a rod with which he could work miracles. What was it called?" The other eight stars all became hysterical—I remember Bill Bixby actually fell out of his chair laughing—and poor little Judy, who had the world's dirtiest mind, had to keep a straight face and try to answer the question.

JoAnne Worley was always a joy to have on the show. Her distinctive personality and charming sense of humor made her one of our most popular panelists. Whenever Heatter/Quigley did a network run through of a celebrity game they were trying to sell, JoAnne was the first person they'd ask to do it. When Bill and I had Marshall-Armstrong Productions, and later, when I put together some presentations on my own, JoAnne was number one on our list of celebrities. That was because she's not only a great game player, but she also has boundless enthusiasm and a wonderful, friendly manner that puts contestants at their ease and pulls the viewer right into the game.

Besides JoAnne and Judy, we used Henry Gibson, Ruth Buzzi, Arte Johnson, Lily Tomlin, Alan Sues, Donna Jean Young, Barbara Sharma, Pamela Rodgers, Teresa Graves, Johnny Brown, Ann Elder, Patti Deutsch, and Eileen Brennan. I guess you could say that *Laugh-In* was the *Hollywood Squares'* best talent pool.

In 1975, we did five special one-hour nighttime shows celebrating the ninth anniversary of *The Hollywood Squares*. Those shows were so much fun. We called them the *Party Shows* and everybody got all dressed up. They brought me these tuxedos to wear and they were so gaudy—all white with fluffy shirts and terrible ties and stuff all over them. I felt like Liberace's worst nightmare. So I asked Art Alisi if it would be okay for me to bring my own tuxedo from home—I had a couple of really nice ones. Well, obviously, they'd made some kind of a deal with a tuxedo company and Art said absolutely not.

Out I came on the first show, feeling very conspicuous in this horrendous suit, and Carl Reiner started to laugh. When I asked him what was so funny, he held up a matchbook and said, "You look like 'Draw Me.'"

Still, the show had an atmosphere none of the other episodes had. I actually wanted to do all the nighttime shows that way, maybe with different tuxedos, but Merrill and Bob didn't agree, so we only did those five one-hour shows. If these shows ever air on the Game Show Network, try to catch them. I'll bet they're as much fun today as they were in 1975.

9

Very Famous Squares

Some very big stars did our show,
and here I tell their tales.

Miss Helen Hayes
October 10, 1900–March 17, 1993

One day I got an unexpected call from *The Mike Douglas Show*. I was told that Helen Hayes was going to be on, and they'd learned that one of her favorite shows was *The Hollywood Squares*. They didn't want to impose, but they thought it would be a nice surprise if I called Miss Hayes during her interview. Impose?! Were they nuts? I was like a nervous little kid waiting to speak to the First Lady of the American Theater. I stood at the phone on my set waiting for the exact moment I was told to call.

Mike Douglas picked up the phone and I identified myself and asked if I could speak to Miss Hayes. He said they had just been talking about me and put her on. So there I was, talking to Helen Hayes on *The Mike Douglas Show,* and she was telling me how much she enjoyed my work. Imagine that! On the spur of the moment, I decided to take a shot and invited her to do *Squares,* and she accepted. She actually ended up doing the show several times and she was a delight. Now, I'm on a first-name basis with most everyone I've met during the course of the show, but there are two stars I would never dream of addressing by their first names. One of them, of course, was Helen Hayes. The other was Gloria Swanson.

Miss Gloria Swanson
March 27, 1899–April 4, 1983

One night I walked into the studio and whose name do I see on a square?

Miss Gloria Swanson. I'm not kidding. It actually said *Miss* Gloria Swanson. I grabbed Mary Markham.

"Mary, you really got Gloria Swanson to do the show?" Well, of course she had, there was the name right in front of my face and I got really excited. I'd been exposed to lots of movie stars and I hardly ever got excited over seeing one, but all my life I'd been listening to my mother talk about two actresses. One was Clara Bow and the other was Gloria Swanson. This was an opportunity to really make my mom happy.

So I rushed to the phone and called her. She wasn't home. I called my house, my sister's house, my kids, everywhere I could think of, and no one knew where Mom was, so I alerted everyone to bring her to the studio as soon as they found her, but not to tell her why.

The thing that surprised me most about Miss Swanson was how diminutive she was. I'd seen her in lots of movies and I never thought of her as being so tiny. When I looked up at her, sitting in a square, I realized why. She had this really large head that made her appear much taller than she was. So here she was, one of the greatest movie stars of all time, sitting in a square with this really large head, and I'm waiting for her to be a real pain in the ass, because I'd heard all kinds of horror stories about the great Miss Swanson. Well, she was a doll. Very sweet and cooperative and a delight to have on the show.

And the whole time I was watching the audience to see if my mom ever showed up, which she didn't. A really good son would have asked to have his picture taken with his mother's favorite actress, or at least gotten an autograph for her, but did I think of it? No! And why would I? Of all the fabulous stars who sat in those boxes, how many autographs do you think I got? If you guessed zero, you get the square. Truthfully, I never even thought of it and it's one of my biggest regrets.

Walter Matthau
October I, 1920–July I, 2000

> Q: What would it mean if you asked a Frenchman to give you satisfaction?
>
> *Walter:* (a pause) This is a dirty show.

I was at La Scala in Beverly Hills one afternoon and who do I spot but Walter Matthau? I knew Walter because we had done a film called *Ensign*

Pulver together. He said, "Hey kid, I like your show. How come you never asked me to be on?"

Well, I was really thrilled. This was Walter Matthau, one of my favorite actors and an Academy Award nominee that year. So I went to Merrill without hesitation and told him excitedly that Walter Matthau wanted to do the show. At the time, everybody wanted to be on *Squares* and Merrill didn't seem that impressed. I couldn't believe it.

"He's nominated for an Oscar," I said.

"Well, tell him to call if he wins," Merrill answered.

Turns out Matthau did win the Oscar for *Fortune Cookie* that year and not too long after, he showed up as one of the guests on the nighttime show. I was delighted to see him.

"Hey, kid," he said, "how much does this show pay?"

"Twelve hundred and fifty dollars," I told him. He was doing nighttime *Squares;* otherwise he would have been getting $750.

"Are you kidding?" he said. "I tip more than that at Orange Julius."

During the course of the show, Walter invited Jay Redack to play in a friendly gin rummy game with some of Hollywood's high rollers. Jay happens to be an excellent gin player, but even so, he decided to try to figure out what the stakes might be. He asked how much he could lose, and Matthau admitted that he was usually the biggest loser.

"I'm not a very good gambler," he said, "but it's never too serious. Nothing you'd really miss." Jay pressed on, asking him how much he had lost in the last game. "Oh, maybe forty-five, fifty thousand," answered Matthau nonchalantly. Jay respectfully declined the invitation.

George C. Scott
October 18, 1927–September 22, 1999

George C. Scott was one of the most revered American actors of this century. He was also an avid golfer and I used to run into him at celebrity golf tournaments every now and then. He was always with his wife, a beautiful actress named Trish Van Devere. Now, George absolutely adored his wife and would have done anything for her. She had a new movie she wanted to plug, and at that time, the two best places to plug a book or movie were *The Tonight Show* or *The Hollywood Squares*. So George suggested he might be willing to do my show if we booked his wife as well. Imagine, George C. Scott, the man who turned down an Oscar, on a game show—*my* game show. This was too good to pass up, even if it was only a one-time deal. Once again I went to Merrill and this time he agreed immediately.

It fell to Harry Friedman, who had recently watched *Patton,* to brief George. He went into the makeup room where George was sitting with his eyes closed, and introduced himself.

"Sit down," barked George, in his Patton-like voice.

Harry sat down immediately and kept his mouth shut while George sat in quiet meditation, eyes still closed. Harry became more and more nervous as the moments crawled by, until finally, George's eyes snapped open and focused on Harry. It was all he could do to keep from fleeing the room.

Then the great man spoke. "I want you to know I'm scared shitless."

"Well, Mr. Scott," said Harry, "that makes two of us."

George ended up having so much fun on the show, he agreed to do it many times, always with his wife, Trish, of course.

George C. Scott, his lovely wife, Trish, and their genial host.

Gene Hackman

Two of my three favorite actors, Walter Matthau and George C. Scott, had already done the show, so when I learned that my other favorite, Gene Hackman, was going to be on the show, I was thrilled. The problem was, our producers had him figured for an intellectual and they gave him some pretty hard questions. Every answer he gave was wrong, and they weren't bluffs, either, just wrong answers. It was killing me because I really didn't want Gene to feel uncomfortable on the show. Of course, he did and there was nothing I could do about it. We had dinner together between shows and I said, "Gene, don't take it so seriously—it's just a game show." But he takes everything seriously. I suppose that's why he's such a great actor.

Years later, I ran into him and he said, "Pete, are you still doing that show?" I told him I wasn't and he said, "Good. That was really a terrible show."

I just read that Gene got involved in a fistfight and decked two young guys because he felt intimidated after a minor traffic accident. As an ex marine, he's a tough guy, so I guess, in retrospect, it could have been worse.

Betty Grable
December 18, 1916–July 3, 1973

I first met Betty Grable when I was about seventeen. I had gone back to Huntington, West Virginia, from New York to finish high school; then I came to Los Angeles to stay with my sister and her husband, Dick Haymes. He was the biggest star at Fox in those days and had done three films with Miss Grable: *Diamond Horseshoe* in 1945, *Do You Love Me?* in 1946, and *The Shocking Miss Pilgrim* in 1947. They became very good friends and remained so until the day she died. I had met Betty at Dick and Joanne's house and she was always very kind and sweet to me, considering she was the biggest movie star of her time and I was her friend's little brother.

Now it's many years later and I'm doing *The Hollywood Squares*. Betty is being managed by Kevin Pines, who was a very close friend of our director, Jerry Shaw. Kevin handled many beautiful women who had once been great stars, among them Jane Russell and Marilyn Maxwell, and he was not only their manager, but also a huge fan. He seemed to know everything about his

Merrill Heatter, me, Abby Dalton, Jackie Vernon, Anne Baxter, Vincent Price, Paul Lynde, Jerry Shaw, Wally Cox, Ed Ames, and Cliff Arquette sing happy birthday to Betty Grable (in the flowered dress) during the dinner break.

clients. One of the best stories he ever told me was about the famous photo of Betty Grable (perhaps the most famous photo from World War II), which one of every five servicemen owned. Her back was to the camera and she was looking over her shoulder in a very sexy pose, but that's not why they took the picture that way. It was because she was several months pregnant at the time. By the way, Kevin said she was wearing a garter on her left leg, but they air-brushed it out because they thought it was a little too risqué. If you happen to know anyone who has a copy of that photo in its original state, let them know it's a real treasure.

At the time, I had a little house on Zuma Beach that I wish I still had today. Patti Page lived on one side of me and Jerry and Kevin on the other. At this point, Betty was very sick with cancer, but she loved to play cards and used to come out on the weekends to play poker. It was hard to believe that the highest-paid woman of 1943, the pinup girl with the million-dollar legs, couldn't get a job and was losing her health insurance. Kevin and Jerry and I conspired to get her on the show, enabling her to make enough money to qualify for health insurance from her union. It was the last job she ever had.

On July 5, 1973, I attended Betty's funeral in Beverly Hills. There was a huge turnout of more than eight hundred people. Her ex-husband, famous bandleader Harry James, actually became physically ill at the funeral and on July 5, 1983, exactly ten years from the date Betty was buried, Harry died.

Ginger Rogers
July 16, 1911–April 25, 1995

In 1994, I was at the wedding of Gary Morton and Susie McCallister in Palm Desert and their neighbor Ginger Rogers was in attendance. At this time, Ginger had been very ill and was in a wheelchair. My wife, Laurie, was very excited to meet her, and Miss Rogers was kind enough to have a picture taken with her. Then Miss Rogers said, "Now I have a favor to ask of you. Do you have a tape of my appearance on *The Hollywood Squares?*"

I have to admit something. So many people did the show that I actually forgot some of them. How I could have forgotten a star like Ginger Rogers, I don't know. Her question completely took me aback. After a little mental prodding, I remembered she had indeed done the show, but I don't think we spoke two words to each other. As I recall, she was a very private person and she was seated in the lox box, so she was hardly called on for the whole show. When I told her all the tapes had been destroyed, she was quite disappointed. It always struck me as odd that, with the body of work this great star had accomplished in her lifetime, she was disappointed because she couldn't get a copy of her appearance on *The Hollywood Squares.*

Andy Kaufman
January 17, 1949–May 16, 1984

When Andy Kaufman was booked to do the show, something happened that had never happened before. His manager, George Shapiro, said the only way Andy would appear on *Hollywood Squares* would be if he could come into the office for his briefing. Andy was a pretty big star, well known for his Latka character on *Taxi*, so Jay and Harry said they would accommodate him. They figured it wouldn't take too long; after all, we normally did it at the studio right before the taping.

Andy and George sat down in Jay's office, and Jay and Harry started telling him the areas of questions, possible bluffs, and joke ideas. Andy just sat there and smiled. Finally, Jay asked if he was making himself clear and Andy responded in Latka gibberish. Jay's an affable fellow, so he laughed and tried again. More Latka gibberish. That's when Jay and Harry realized they weren't briefing Andy Kaufman at all—they were briefing Latka. An hour went by and the guys could see they were getting nowhere, so Jay turned to George and told him it wasn't going to work. George took Latka out in the hall, and when they came back, he was Andy. The rest of the briefing went fine. Later, George told Jay it was the only time he'd ever seen Andy break character in the middle of a meeting.

Well, Andy did the show, and at the dinner break he came to me and said, "I hope I'm not driving you too crazy with what I do." I told him to go ahead and do his thing. I was actually enjoying it. The problem was, viewers interpreted Kaufman's shtick as an attack on me, and NBC received so much hate mail, mostly defending me against Andy, that they made the decision never to use him again.

Sammy Davis Jr.
December 8, 1925–May 16, 1990

I met Sammy Davis Jr. when we were kids. We used to hang around in Hollywood at Coffee Dan's on Vine Street. Sammy was working with his father and his uncle in a group called the Will Mastin Trio, and they lived in a black hotel called The American. I guess they were making about $500 a week. In 1949 or 1950, my partner, Tommy Noonan, and I opened for Frances Langford at a place called Tahoe Village at the beginning of the season. Jimmy Durante was scheduled to close the season that year, but for some reason he fell out, and they hired us to take his place. We had to bring in an opening act, so we hired the Will Mastin Trio for $750. In those days, blacks weren't allowed to stay in the same motels or eat in the same restaurants as whites. Now that I think about it, I don't know where they stayed. Nothing was on the South Shore but a bowling alley; a couple of restaurants, Tahoe Village and The Wagon Wheel; and a couple of other little gambling joints. So the Trio stayed in the motel with us, ate where

Sammy Davis
Jr. and me,
horsing
around in
his suite.

we ate, went bowling with us, and worked as our opening act on many occasions.

Then Sammy became a huge star and didn't talk to me for many years. To this day, I still don't have any idea why. But one day I was sitting in a bar in London and in walks Sammy. He came over and put his arms around me and said, "I'm sorry, man."

On his fiftieth anniversary in show biz, Sammy did ten special nights at Harrah's in Tahoe. Every night he brought in an act that was very important to his life. I was invited to open for him on one of those nights, and he introduced me by giving me a big Sammy hug and saying, "This is the guy who first got the Will Mastin Trio into white motels and restaurants." That was a great moment for me.

Sammy, The Chapter Five, me, and Florence Henderson.

Dolly Parton

I'll never forget the first time Dolly did our show. It was a nighttime taping and we had a cast change after the first three shows. Everybody was in
the dinner hall and in walks this woman. She had high, high heels; huge
bleached blond hair; a little tiny waist; a ton of makeup; and the biggest
breasts I'd ever seen. Everybody's fork stopped in mid-bite. Dolly just smiled

and said, "Hi, everybody, I'm Dolly." She fluffed her hair and everything jiggled. "Bet you think I'm wearing a wig, don't you? Well, stop by my dressing room and I'll show you. This is the real thing."

Dolly felt guilty because she thought she didn't play the game very well, but I thought she was adorable. My stepdaughter, Gaby, was fourteen years old at the time, and her ambition was to be a singer. She actually had a great voice, good enough for me to spring for a demo tape of her songs. Dolly was one of Gaby's idols—Gaby played Dolly's albums all day long and even recorded one of Dolly's songs on her tape. That was about the time the movie *Nine to Five* was in production, so I took a chance and brought Gaby to the movie set to see if she could meet Dolly in person.

Well, Lily Tomlin, Jane Fonda, and Dabney Coleman were there, but Gaby couldn't have been less interested, and when she finally met Dolly, it was as if nobody else existed. Dolly was as sweet and gracious as she could be and even promised to listen to the demo tape that Gaby had hopefully brought with her. Dolly even said she'd call after she heard it to let Gaby know what she thought.

Poor Gaby sat by the phone every minute after that. The first words out of her mouth when she came home from school were, "Did Dolly call?" I tried to explain that Dolly Parton was a very busy person. She wasn't going to take the time to call a teenager. But Gaby just mooned around the telephone, waiting for it to ring. It was kind of sad and funny at the same time.

Then one day the phone rang. I could hardy believe it was Dolly calling for Gaby, who still remembers the conversation, word for word.

"Hello, star," said Dolly. "You sound like a cross between me, Barbra Streisand, and Linda Ronstadt."

After that, Gaby was really Dolly-struck. Whenever Dolly did *The Tonight Show*, I'd take Gaby to the studio and she'd go backstage and talk to her. Over time, they got friendly enough for Gaby to feel comfortable calling her on her own. Dolly invited her to the set of *The Best Little Whorehouse in Texas* and a couple of years later to the filming of *Rhinestone*.

By now, Gaby was seventeen and decided to ask Dolly to go to dinner. Now, I really laughed, but Dolly said she'd love to and three days later a limo pulled up in front of the house to pick up Gaby. Dolly took her to the set to watch dailies, then to dinner at Stanleys, a trendy restaurant in Sherman

My step-daughter Gaby with Dolly Parton and me in front of Dolly's *Nine to Five* trailer.

Oaks, not far from Encino, where we lived. It was the biggest night of Gaby's teenage life. Well, maybe there was one exception.

Nine to Five was premiering just before Christmas and Gaby begged us to get her a ticket for her Christmas present. That was all she wanted. I explained to her that Paul Lynde was having a Christmas party that same night, and I'd already told him we would be there, so it was impossible to go to the premiere. I piled the trunk full of gifts for Paul and others and we set out for the party with a very disappointed Gaby in tow. As we drove through Hollywood, we noticed a huge crowd in front of a theater.

"Let's see what all this is about," I said and parked the car. Well, I'd had tickets for the premiere all along and Gaby got so excited, she started to cry. The press was there and they interviewed us, with Gaby crying like a baby. Then Dolly came over to join us and the reporter said to her, "This is Peter Marshall's stepdaughter. He surprised her by bringing her here to meet you and it made her cry." Dolly looked over at Gaby and said to her, "He's talking to me like I don't know you."

Milton Berle
July 12, 1908–March 27, 2002

It was very early on and Milton Berle was booked to do the show. Art Alisi came to me in a panic. "Milton is refusing to do the show. He's very unhappy with his dressing room. Is there anything you can do?"

Very Famous Squares

Now, I'd known Milton since I was thirteen years old. His first wife, Joyce Matthews, and my sister, Joanne, were in a show called *Hold on to Your Hats* together. The star of that show was none other than the great Al Jolson, who fell madly in love with my sister, but that's another story. So I went to Milton and I said, "I understand you're unhappy. What seems to be the problem?"

"Look at this dressing room," he yelled. "I've been working at this studio for my whole life, and I know there are a lot better dressing rooms than this one."

Milton Berle had to be cajoled, but it was worth it.

"You're absolutely right," I answered. "I have no idea why you're doing this show. It's only a game show. You're a very big star, Milton. You don't need this. Why don't you go home?"

This stopped Milton in his tracks. "Well, why would I do that?"

"Because you're unhappy."

"I'm a professional," he said.

"But if you're unhappy, I can call JoAnne Worley or Dick Patterson or Bob Fuller. They all live in Toluca Lake. Or I can go down the hall—I'll find somebody."

"What are you talking about?" he said. "I've never walked out on a commitment in my life. I brought five suits and I'm doing the show."

"Okay, Milton. Whatever you want." I walked back to the set where Art Alisi waited impatiently.

"Don't worry about a thing," I told him. "Milton's doing the show."

"What did you say to him?"

"Nothing really—but he's doing the show."

Once Milton had calmed down, Les Roberts went in to give him his jokes. Milton looked them over and grabbed Les by the lapel. "Do you swear to God this got a laugh the first time it was used?" When Les told him the joke was brand new, written especially for him, he refused to do it.

Alice Cooper

My kids very seldom went to the studio. Everybody else's kids loved to come to tapings, but the only time I could get any of my kids to go was when we did *Storybook Squares*, and then Jaime was the only one who was young enough to enjoy it. Sometimes I thought they were embarrassed to be associated with the show and maybe even with me. Then one day I announced that Alice Cooper was going to be on. Well, all of a sudden it was, "Gee, Dad, I sure would like to come down to the studio and watch you do your thing." And, "I thought maybe I'd drop by the studio tonight. Maybe we could have dinner."

I really didn't want to bug a big rock star like Alice Cooper, so I told my kids they were welcome to come to the taping, but not to be pushy about asking for autographs or photos, and they promised they'd behave.

Peter LaCock, David LaCock, Alice Cooper, Jaime LaCock, and me. It didn't take much to make my kids happy—just having their picture taken with a world-famous rock star.

Turned out that Alice was as excited about being on the show as my kids were about seeing him there. He came wearing a "Peter Marshall's Fan Club" T-shirt he'd had made for himself and he brought one along for everybody else.

In their pictures with him, you can see by my kids' faces that Alice had no problem giving them autographs and spending a little time schmoozing with them, which made it a *very* big night in their lives.

Glenn Ford

Glenn Ford was the first big movie star ever booked on the show and for whatever reason, he loved to do *The Hollywood Squares*. In those days, it seemed like people drank a lot more than they do today and Glenn was no exception. He wasn't very good at the game, so when he was booked, we usually put him in the lox box.

The first time he was on the show, because of the way the tic-tac-toe game went, he didn't get called on for two entire shows, and he went into a huge depression because he thought no one remembered him anymore and his career was over.

Glenn was positively paranoid about looking stupid, so we always gave him questions about movies or guns or the military, or questions that could be answered true or false.

We once asked him, "True or false? To keep nylon stockings from running, you should store them in the freezer." Glenn, always very prickly about his masculine image, said, "How should I know? Ask Cesar Romero!"

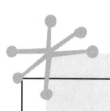

10

Pegging the Squares

My take on many of the stars: my favorite,
my least favorite, the funniest, the sexiest,
and on and on.

It seems no matter how many years go by since the first *Hollywood Squares* was on the air, people still ask me about the celebrities who did the show. Who did I like the best? Who did I not like at all? Who was the funniest, the sexiest, the most lovable? Well, I've given these questions a lot of thought and this is the way I remember it.

George Gobel, as I said earlier, was my favorite square of all time. His funny, laid-back attitude made me scream and he was so sweet. I guess I just loved the guy.

Here's George on *The Peter Marshall Variety Show*. I don't think I ever looked at either of my first two wives quite like that.

My least favorite square was Jackie Mason. I think the reason he was so tough was the same reason he was on the show in the first place—because he was a comic. You'd think the funnier the star was, the better panelist he or she would be, but this was about as far from the truth as you could get. I would ask Jackie a question and that would start him on a three- or four-minute rant. I'd try to bring him back on track, but he'd ignore me and keep going for a long, drawn-out gag.

Sometimes I'd ask another star a question and Jackie would answer from his square, or come up with a quick joke that really stepped on the selected star's line. Hearing a disembodied voice is very confusing to the home viewer, so when Jackie would start, Jerry Shaw would have to try to get a camera on him, leaving the star who was legitimately answering the question. Sometimes, by the time he'd get there, Jackie had finished and the other star had started talking again. This made directing the show a lot harder than it had to be.

Me, Rose Marie, Tony Randall, Shelley Fabares, George Gobel, Dennis Weaver, Susan Clark, Jack Albertson, Paul Lynde, and Robert Goulet, all on the eleventh anniversary of *The Hollywood Squares*.

Not that Jackie was the only one who did this. A lot of the comedians we used, some of the people I personally find hilarious, couldn't play the game for the very same reason—they couldn't resist pushing for jokes and they couldn't keep their mouths shut.

So I would patiently explain this to Jackie and he'd nod his head as if to tell me he understood. Then I'd ask a question, not even to him, and you'd hear his voice interrupting the question or deriding the joke. As good as Jackie Mason is on stage, that's how bad he was on *Squares*, and that's why he was my least favorite square of all time.

Now that doesn't mean he was the biggest pain in the ass. That honor went, unequivocally, to Tony Randall. Don't get me wrong. I really did, and still do, love Tony with all my heart, but one night he was so busy being his droll, intelligent self, he absolutely would not get to the answer. It was one of the rare times I lost my patience on the show and I said, "Tony, you're a pain in the ass." After the taping, Tony came to me and said, "Pete, you never should have said that to me on the air." Well, I thought about this, and of course, Tony was right, so I said, "I apologize. You're right, I never should have said that on the air—but you're still a pain in the ass."

The best bluffer I ever saw, and everybody agrees on this, was Robert Fuller. I'd ask him a question. After his answer, I'd be so sure he was right, I'd barely glance at the card. When I'd look down and see that his answer was totally wrong, I was always amazed.

The worst bluffer was Kaye Ballard. She was so sweet, she didn't want any of the contestants to lose, so if she tried to bluff, she'd actually end up telling them she was bluffing.

On that note, I think the most guilt-ridden square must have been Peter Falk. One time he was the Secret Square and he answered the question wrong. The contestant agreed with him. He felt so bad about being the

She looked tough on *Storybook Squares*, but Kaye Ballard was a pussycat when it came to the contestants.

cause of that person losing the game and a lot of money, he never would come on the show again.

The sexiest woman who was ever on the show, bar none, was Diana Rigg. She showed up wearing a little T-shirt with the word "Tits" written across her chest. You know how some people just give off an aura that's irresistible to the opposite sex? Double it, and you'll be getting close to the way Diana Rigg affected me. During the entire run of *Squares*, I never fooled around with anybody on the show, either star or contestant. The one time I seriously considered trying was when Diana was on. And you know what? I'm kind of sorry I didn't.

The saddest square, to me, was young Mackenzie Phillips, daughter of John Phillips of *The Mamas and the Papas* and one of the stars of the hit show *One Day at a Time*. I'd go looking for her between shows and find her passed out on the couch in her dressing room. I couldn't figure out how she was going to get up for the next show, but she always did. I found out later, while watching her story on *Biography*, that during that time she was relying 100 percent on drugs to keep her going. Mackenzie has long since straightened herself out, and I couldn't be happier for her. She's made a hard-earned comeback and is doing a good job raising her son, but having two daughters myself, it just broke my heart to see her during the days when she did *The Hollywood Squares*.

Mackenzie Phillips just broke my heart.

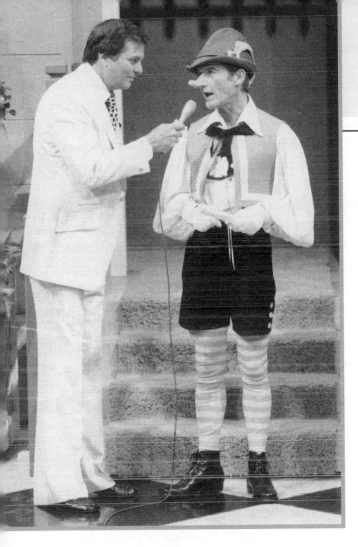

Here's Roddy McDowall as Pinocchio on *Storybook Squares*. He'd rather tell a lie than hurt anyone's feelings.

The most lovable square by far was Roddy McDowall. His best friend was Elizabeth Taylor and we used to do terrible jokes about her. Most of these jokes came from Joan Rivers. She'd say things like "Elizabeth Taylor has more chins than a Chinese phone book" or "I always try to be at McDonald's when Elizabeth Taylor is ordering lunch. I like to watch the numbers change" or "Elizabeth Taylor is the only woman who stares at a microwave oven and yells, 'Hurry up!'" Once I asked Joan this question: "At a recent Hollywood auction, something was sold that Liz Taylor used a lot in the movie *Cleopatra*. What was it?" Her answer: "Rex Harrison." Roddy would cringe at these remarks because he knew Elizabeth watched the show.

Sure enough, after the show Elizabeth would call Roddy, and it was clear her feelings were hurt and he would feel just terrible. Joan was also a very close friend of Roddy's; in fact, he was godfather to Joan's daughter Melissa. She knew exactly what she was doing when she made all those Elizabeth Taylor jokes, but no matter how much she pushed Roddy's buttons, he would never say anything to her about laying off Elizabeth. I guess he didn't want to hurt Joan's feelings either.

The funniest square, hands down, was Mel Brooks. I'd come in early, see Mel's name on one of the boxes, and start to laugh. One time when Mel was doing the show, Merrill went to the Beverly Hills Hotel, where Mel and his wife were staying, to brief him. After they'd gone over the questions, they kibitzed for a while, and then Mel said, "Hey, want to see a movie star sleeping?" With that, he tiptoed to the door of the bedroom, opened it and motioned for Merrill to look in. There was Anne Bancroft, fast asleep. Merrill didn't even mention that he'd seen his own movie-star wife, the former Elaine Stewart, sleeping thousands of times.

I loved my sister's sweatshirt, especially since I'd always been known as Joanne Dru's brother.

Don Rickles was also a very funny square, but I can't say he was as funny as Mel Brooks. Instead, I'd say he was the most spontaneous square. We never wrote jokes for Don, or even went over questions with him. We just let him wing it. Here are a couple that really made me laugh.

Q: What is another name for the game of ping-pong?
Don: Hit the ball, Bruce.

Q: What is the national sport of Canada?
Don: How should I know? They knock a hole in the ice and fish!

That one brought a lot of angry letters from our viewers north of the border.

The square I loved the most was my sister, Joanne Dru. It was very tough for me to get my sister on the show. First of all, she hated doing appearances, except as an actress. And, of course, I ran into the same old problem with Merrill. Joanne wasn't his idea of a great booking. But in all the years we were both in the business, I never had an opportunity to work with my sister and I really wanted to do that. So I bugged Merrill and I bugged Joanne and in 1967, she did the show. She did it again in 1975 when she was one of fifty-three celebrity panelists to do five special one-hour editions celebrating the ninth anniversary of the show.

The longest-winded square is a tie. Chad Everett did a monologue about Mrs. Lincoln's hairy legs that went on forever and it was so funny. And Maureen O'Hara had a story about the banshees, those creatures from Irish folklore who howl before someone dies. When the stars got on a roll and the story was really entertaining, I used to let them go. I figured Jerry could fix it in editing if he wanted to. On those shows, we often didn't get in as many questions as Merrill and Bob liked, but the trade-off for laughter was well worth it.

The square with the least understanding of how to play the game? That would be the great Groucho Marx. He just didn't get it. He thought he had to talk all the time, to save us from dead air, but he was Groucho and it was an honor to have him on, so when the show was over, I said, "Thank you so much for doing the show. I hope you'll do it again someday." He said, "Son, the only time I'd like to see you again is socially."

The trouble with Groucho was he had too much to say.

The square I was the least close to? Gypsy Rose Lee. She did the show many, many times, but I never felt I got to know her. She kept to herself, never socialized with the rest of us, and never accepted the invitations to go on any of the trips we took. The only thing I really remember about Gypsy was that she always used to take food home from our catered dinners. She said it was for her dogs, which it may or may not have been. I understand that attitude about wasting food. I'm never comfortable unless my pantry is full. It's a depression mentality that comes from living through a time when you never knew if there would be food on the table tomorrow, and if you've never lived through it, you'll never really understand what it's like. When Gypsy died, her sister, June Havoc, was very upset that the folks from *Squares* didn't pay more attention to Gypsy during her illness, but the truth of the matter is, we didn't even know she was ill.

The most rambunctious square was Robert Goulet. Whenever he was seated in the top row, he loved to start rocking the set, like a kid on a Ferris wheel. Everybody would yell for him to stop, but that only made him swing it all the harder. I know I keep saying this, but back then we all drank a lot more and partied a lot harder, and most of us were much cruder. Robert

Goulet, Leslie Nielsen, and Burt Reynolds used to go over to the Carriage House for drinks, spend a lot of time punching each other on the upper arms, and take bets to see who could get the cocktail waitress's phone number first. Somehow it didn't seem as obnoxious then as it would today.

On the other hand, the most charming square, always a perfect gentleman, was matinee idol Ricardo Montalban, also known for the 1970s TV show *Fantasy Island*. He played the game well, was never disruptive, and

Ricardo Montalban adding a touch of class to a
panel that already looks pretty darn good.

WALLY COX · SALLY ANN HOWES · ARTE JOHNSON

BURT REYNOLDS · PAUL LYNDE · LILY TOMLIN

CHARLEY WEAVER · KATHY GARVER · RICARDO MONTALBAN

Jacqueline Susann, Pat Henry, Vincent Price, Shirley Jones, Rose Marie, Wally, Paul, Cliff, and Jack Cassidy, all holding each other up. Must have been right after the dinner break.

brought a certain class to the whole show. Because he was such a delight, we asked Mary Markham to try to get us these kinds of bookings more often. I guess she thought we were referring to his ethnic background rather than his personality, because we immediately had a flood of Hispanic entertainers. Whenever Quig would show up at the studio and see one of these guys, he'd wave his hands around and say, "Jesus Christ, not another one of those Ricardo characters."

The most egotistical square was Jack Cassidy. Jack was doing *Superman* on Broadway at the same time I was doing *Skyscraper*. We got to know each other quite well and he really was a dichotomy: extremely handsome and very egotistical, but funny. In fact, I've never met a funnier leading man than Jack. He also cut a pretty wide swath through the women of New York, before he got really lucky and married Shirley Jones.

Jack didn't want to do *The Hollywood Squares* because he was afraid he'd get an answer wrong and look dumb, and this didn't tie in with his image of himself. NBC had some very strict rules about how the stars were to be briefed on the questions before the show. Whoever was doing the briefing would tell them they were going to be asked a question about World War II, or gnats, or strawberries, but the specific question was never divulged and the answers were kept top secret. This just wouldn't do for Jack, and he managed to work something out with our producer, Bill Armstrong. They were good friends, so it wasn't unusual for them to have lunch together, even on the day of a taping. That night, Jack would get every answer right. It didn't really matter much, since the contestant only had to agree or disagree—but it mattered to Jack. He hated being wrong.

Jack and Shirley had split up by then, and Jack was living in an apartment on Kings Road in West Hollywood. I was divorced from Nadine and on the loose, so I saw quite a bit of Jack during that time. He was a strange guy, but sort of like a magnet—he drew people to him. One night I came into the studio knowing Jack was booked on the show and looking forward to seeing him. His name wasn't on a square and Vicki Casper was crying. I knew something terrible had happened even before she told me the news. Jack had died in a fire in his apartment. This was heartbreaking to me because I enjoyed him so much, not only as a talent but also as a good friend.

The "butchest" square? It's right there in his nickname, Cesar "Butch" Romero. I had known Cesar since 1943 when I was a kid at Fox and he was

Two of my idols: Cesar Romero and Buddy Rogers.

this dashing Latin leading man. There were always all kinds of rumors about whether he was gay or straight, but I couldn't have cared less because he was always so charming and so nice to everyone.

He was on the show one night and seemed to be quite depressed, so I asked him what was wrong. He told me it was his sixtieth birthday. "But you look like you're forty. Why would you of all people worry about being sixty?"

"When you get to be my age, Pete, you look at your life in decades. That means the next birthday I'm looking at is seventy—and that's depressing."

When I turned sixty I thought about Cesar. I just hope I live as long and healthy a life as he did. He lived to be an amazingly young and good-looking eighty-six. That's not depressing!

The shortest square was Michael Dunn, the talented dwarf actor best known as Dr. Miguelito Loveless on the 1960s TV show *The Wild Wild West*. I had met him when he played my son in my very first Broadway play, *How to Make a Man*. Not only was he a great actor even then, he was also a wonderful singer. I was delighted when he showed up to be on *Squares*.

When he walked into the studio, Quig became very agitated. "I didn't know he was *that* short!" We explained that it didn't matter how short he was. He was going to sit on cushions in the square, anyway, but Quig asked Les Roberts to get him out of his dressing room so the prop people could look at him and figure out how many cushions would be needed. "But be discreet," Quig said. "Quig," Les replied, "he knows how short he is." Dunn, a delightful guy, complied, but first said, "Let's not use cushions at all. I can be the Invisible Man."

The sleepiest square had to be Jack Palance. When he showed up on the set he didn't greet anyone, and just let it be known that he wanted a drink. Well, Merrill and Bob never had any liquor on the set, only wine with dinner. If anyone wanted a drink with their dinner, they'd have to go across the street to Chadney's to eat, which a lot of stars (and production staff) did. But *nobody* drank before the dinner break. Merrill explained this. Palance glared at him and said, "I want a drink *now!*" It's the only time I ever saw Merrill Heatter back down. Glenn Ford was on the show that night and he always carried a briefcase full of booze, so I guess he and Palance shared.

I don't think Jack's heart was really in this appearance. Every time we'd ask him a question, he'd grunt his answer in a monosyllable. Finally, a contestant called on him during the fourth show. I asked the question and got no answer at all. I looked up to find Jack Palance fast asleep. I gestured to Michael Landon, who was sitting next to him, to wake him up. Michael shook his head vehemently. Later he said, "No way I was going to wake him up! I was afraid he'd bite my neck."

The star who enjoyed being on the show the least, I think, was George Sanders. George was a great actor, a brilliant man, and an absolute delight. He used to write limericks about people he either liked a lot, or didn't like at all. I still remember one he wrote about Lawrence Harvey, who was not one of his favorites.

This is me as a robot in *How to Make a Man.* Michael Dunn played my son, and Barbara Britton, who went on to become Mrs. North in the *Mr. and Mrs. North* TV series, played my wife.

Hark to the tale of know-it-all Larry,

A cross between Shakespeare and Madame DuBarry,

With the vices of both and the talents of neither

He says to the world, you can have me as either.

One time Jerry Shaw went to George with the camera and there he was, sitting in his box reading *Time* magazine. Then there was the time our writers loaded him up with lots of jokes and questions about his ex-wife, Zsa Zsa Gabor. They had no idea he had married Zsa Zsa's sister, Magda, just a few weeks earlier. Coupled with the fact that he'd recently suffered a minor stroke, I'm sure that show wasn't the most fun he'd ever had.

In 1972, we were all saddened to hear that George's body was discovered in a hotel in Barcelona next to five empty bottles of Nembutal. Eloquent to the end, his note read, "Dear World, I am leaving because I am bored. I feel I have lived long enough. I am leaving you with your worries in this sweet cesspool. Good luck."

The most glamorous square was Zsa Zsa Gabor. You need to understand that at NBC we had the finest hair and makeup people in the world. Zsa Zsa, however, would insist on bringing her own makeup artist and hairdresser. Their cost was much higher than Zsa Zsa's salary for the show. She would also always ask for a limousine to pick her up and bring her to the studio. The driver would have to wait through the whole taping, about five hours, at the show's expense. Now here comes the best part. Just before the first show, Zsa Zsa would become very upset. "Dahling," she would say, "I've forgotten my false eyelashes. I can't possibly be seen on television without them."

No matter how we would try to persuade Zsa Zsa that the false eyelashes the studio already had in their makeup room were the best money could buy, she would insist her driver be sent out to pick up her favorite brand. Off he would go, with a studio voucher, and back he would come with ten pairs of lashes for Zsa Zsa—at $150 a set. Now that's glamour!

The dirtiest square was a little black puppet named Jiffy. She accompanied Wayland & Madame, but she got away with more on the show than anyone else ever did. Maybe she could get past the censors because she wasn't a real person; I don't know, but that little puppet sure made me laugh.

I fell in love with Wayland & Madame when I was getting ready to do *The Peter Marshall Variety Show.* Merv Griffin used to have a fan who came to every taping and sat in the front row. Her name was Mrs. Miller and she became part of his show. I was looking at tapes and I happened to see this wonderful act that I thought would be perfect to be my "Mrs. Miller." I planned to do a little monologue with them every week and Madame would have been my biggest fan. So I told Mary Markham, who did all the bookings for *Squares,* about my idea, but I was too late. She was booking *The Andy Williams Show* at the time and Madame was already Andy's biggest fan.

I would have loved to have had Wayland & Madame on *The Hollywood Squares,* but since it seemed like it was death for anyone I suggested for the show, I decided to just talk them up surreptitiously. As I mentioned earlier, Paul had developed a relationship with Wayland when he was on his own tour, and I think he was the one who was finally instrumental in getting them on the show. Of all the newcomers to the show, they probably had the greatest impact. I would do a warm-up with Wayland & Madame that was never scripted and would go on for about fifteen minutes. People screamed with laughter the whole time. Now believe me, I am not that funny, so obvi-

Wayland Flowers & Madame always got the audience laughing. Madame was crude, but Wayland's other puppet, Jiffy, was downright filthy.

ously it was Madame. Wayland was a very polite Southern gentleman and Madame was the filthiest, bawdiest, rudest thing in the world, and that contrast was what made the act so great. You would never watch him—your eyes were always on her. Then Wayland started introducing new characters. That's when we had the pleasure of meeting Jiffy. Wayland was really a genius and one of the most talented guys I ever knew.

The longest-running square was Rose Marie. She did the first pilot with Bert Parks, the second pilot with Sandy Baron, and the first and last network episodes of the show.

The longest-winded square? No contest: Mickey Rooney. I used to say, "Let me know when he gets to the studio," and then I would hide. Even though Mickey was really short, he was one of these guys who would come right up to you and talk into your face. He would talk about the operas he was writing and the poetry he was reading and the restaurants he was buying and the theater he was designing. Although it was all very interesting and funny, and most of the staff loved listening to him, I didn't have time to banter with Mickey Rooney. So I learned to just say "Hi, Mick" and keep on going whenever he did the show.

Who's the one person I wish could have been a Hollywood Square? Easy. That would be Greta Garbo. Unfortunately, it never happened. I think it was a *Time* survey that listed the most unlikely words you'll ever hear as, "Greta Garbo to block." But once, when Greta Garbo was staying in Beverly Hills with Gaylord Hauser, she visited my sister, who lived right across the street. She spotted a picture of me on the wall and asked Joanne, "Do you know this boy?"

"That's my brother," Joanne answered. "Do you know him?"

"No," said Miss Garbo, "but I watch him on television every day. I just love his show."

Wouldn't it have been an amazing thing if someone had had the guts to invite Greta Garbo to be on a game show and she had said yes? Just something I like to think about now and then.

11

Storybook Squares

The most fun I ever had doing television.

Everybody loved doing *Storybook Squares*—well, almost everybody. Paul Lynde actually hated it when he had to play the Wicked Witch. First of all, he had to sit through a long makeup session in which they'd make him look really bad, with a twisted hook nose and black moles sticking out of his face. Then we'd hook up a green light in his square, giving him a terrible pallor. While I never would have called Paul a truly handsome man, he was very vain and hated to be made to look ugly. Every time he'd catch a glimpse of himself in the monitor, he'd cringe. Of course, Paul was also not a big

What a great set, and lots of fun when the families played.

fan of children and we didn't let any of the celebs drink during the *Storybook Squares* tapings because there were children on the set—two more reasons for Paul not to be wild about the show. I think he kind of enjoyed it when he played Davy Crockett or Paul Bunyan, though.

Abby Dalton, on the other hand, loved playing the Wicked Witch. When she saw herself in full makeup, she called her housekeeper and asked her to bring her kids right over. She figured they would really enjoy this. So there she was, with green skin and a big wart on her nose with a hair coming out of it, and in walk her three kids. They were just little tykes at the time. Abby let loose with a blood-curdling witch laugh and those kids took off so fast, I think they ran all the way home before the housekeeper even got to the car. It really helped Abby keep them on their best behavior for a very long time, though. All she had to do was start to cackle, and those kids really toed the line.

We loved to book actors who played a specific character to play that character on our show. For instance, Bill Shatner came on as Captain Kirk and it was the only time he'd ever appeared on television in his *Star Trek* uni-

That's my daughter Jaime and one of her pals on a visit to the show.

Joan Rivers as
Little Red Riding
Hood and me as the
Big Bad Wolf.

form, except on *Star Trek*, of course. We wanted to book Leonard Nimoy as Mr. Spock, but Quig said, "Only if he wears the ears. He doesn't mean anything to anybody without the ears."

Some characters appeared on *Storybook Squares* many times, with different people playing the parts. There was more than one wicked witch, more than one Little Red Riding Hood, and as many Tarzans as we could find. The women loved it when we had Tarzan, because he always wore his loincloth. Ted Cassidy appeared as Tarzan, but the most memorable Tarzan was definitely Ron Ely, from the TV series. He not only wore his loincloth, but he also brought his chimp. Unfortunately, nature called at exactly the wrong moment.

Whoever was sitting next to Ron started to laugh, so the chimp thought he was being funny and proceeded to rub his feces all over the microphone, the tables, the chairs. Well, you can't even begin to imagine the stench that arose. The kids who were contestants tried their best to keep playing the

Charo as Tarzan's Jane.

game, but it wasn't easy for them to concentrate. The stars tried to answer the questions and look like they were having a good time, but every time we took a break, everybody wanted to run for their lives.

Anyone who ever saw *Storybook Squares* agreed it was brilliantly done. Each star would be dressed as a famous character and we'd have a lot of fun casting them as their exact opposites. Besides making Paul some macho character or other, we'd cast Leslie Uggams as Snow White, Judy Carne as Goldilocks, and Arte Johnson as his Tyrone F. Horneigh character (called

"The Nice Old Man" for show purposes). Arte, a serious actor, was always deep in character while in costume, and downstairs in the dressing room area he goosed every man, woman, and child who walked by him, including a group of Japanese tourists. Charo once played Rapunzel wearing a long, black wig, and she looked so good that Joan Rivers suggested she become a brunette.

The show was cleverly written and the costumes were magnificent. Each star would be ushered through the arch on stage by a pageboy and I would introduce them. Then they would go to their squares and we'd have a little business; for instance, Paul, as the Evil Queen, would look into his mirror and sing "I feel pretty, oh so pretty, I feel pretty and witty and *gayayayay.*"

Here's Arte Johnson as Thomas Edison and one of our contestants with her mom. Hard to believe that little girl is now in her forties.

We'd put the reverb on the *gayayayay,* followed by the sound of the mirror breaking. And when Arte Johnson was Abraham Lincoln wearing a hat that was five feet tall, we'd play *Hail to the Chief* and follow it with a gunshot and the sound of feet running away. It really was a very hip show. By the time we finished all that and I introduced the kids who were the contestants, we had about eight minutes left to play the game. I think that's why the show ultimately failed. If it had been an hour long, we would have had time to do all the peripheral stuff and still get a decent game with a good number of questions in, and I really believe *Storybook Squares* would have been a huge success.

We had some fun reviving it during special theme weeks once in a while, but the show was only on the air for eight months. Unlike the daytime shows, we did rerun them. They were so expensive, I suppose that was the only way to make back the money.

12

Friendships and Romances

Some of the relationships that grew on the show, plus a plain old one-night stand.

It was always fun to watch a female star who was doing the show for the very first time. For instance, the first time Phyllis Diller was a guest, she showed up with five fabulous outfits with matching shoes, accessories, and jewelry. Rose Marie was her roommate and she watched, hands on hips, as Phyllis unpacked her finery. When Phyllis finally finished putting everything away, Ro raised an eyebrow and asked, "Are you going to put in a pool, too?" That's when Phyllis realized that Ro had brought five tops and one pair of old jeans. Since nobody ever saw the stars below the waist on the show, it didn't really matter. When the weather was warm, I did many shows wearing a dress shirt, tie, jacket, and a pair of shorts.

Phyllis became a regular and I loved watching her get comfortable with the show and the other members of the panel. One night, she shared a dressing room with Margaret Truman, whom she had never met before. They learned that they had both studied operatic singing and were both sopranos, and they got along famously. When I spoke with Phyllis recently, she told me she and Margaret have remained fast friends and still see each other regularly.

Karen Valentine was on the show the first time Ethel Merman did it, and ended up sharing a dressing room with her. Well, Ethel was Karen's idol, so Karen couldn't have been more excited. After the first show, Ethel complimented Karen on how at ease and professional she was, and confessed that she personally was a nervous wreck. When Karen asked how a consummate pro like Merman could be nervous doing a little game show, Ethel said, "Hell, honey, there's no script. I'd sure hate to disappoint my audience."

The flimflam man with a couple of great broads, Ethel Merman and Tammy Wynette.

Well, Karen knew everything about Merman and paraphrased one of her own famous lines back at her: "If they could do what you can do, they'd be up here and you'd be out there." Ethel ended up having a great time on the show and came back to do it many times. And she and Karen remained friends until Ethel's death in 1984.

The group from *The Hollywood Squares* took a lot of trips together and I'll tell you about them in a bit, but we also hung out a lot at home. Sometimes, after a taping, everybody was a little too wound up to go right home, so we'd go out and have a drink and talk a little, until we came down. I remember one night when we had a particularly good group on the show. Somebody mentioned that a new topless bar had opened on Van Nuys Boulevard in the San Fernando Valley, and suggested it would be fun to go. Now this was unusual at the time, because they didn't have topless bars in that part of the

This *Storybook Squares* panel features Jim Backus, Ted Cassidy, Paul Winchell, JoAnne Worley, Wally Cox, Elke Sommer, Cliff Arquette, Judy Carne, and Mike Landon. Cliff and Mike had it easy as Charley Weaver and Little Joe.

I'm just astounded that I finally had the foresight to bring a camera to the studio and get somebody to take these pictures for me. I was thrilled when I found them in my collection.

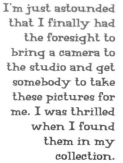

Above: Paul Lynde as the Evil Queen.

Left: Paul Lynde as Paul Bunyan.

George Gobel as
Little Boy Blue.

Leslie Uggams as
Snow White.

Doc Severinsen as the Angel Gabriel, Bonnie Franklin as
Peter Pan, Roddy McDowell as Sherlock Holmes, William
Shatner as Captain Kirk, and Julie McWhirter as Dorothy.

Rose Marie went bananas on our *Hollywood Squares* trip to Jamaica.

Jonathan Winters breaking everyone up, including Karen Valentine and Paul Lynde.

Rue McClanahan and Rita Moreno getting down on the beach in Jamaica.

If you like piña coladas, then you're just like Jonathan Winters.

Leslie Uggams and
me, ready to take
the plunge.

valley, so a bunch of us headed for it. It was Karen Valentine and her husband, Lily Tomlin and her manager, Nanette Fabray and her husband, Rose Marie, Cliff Arquette, Wally Cox, Bill Armstrong and his wife, Paul Lynde, and me. We walked in and were really surprised to see these young, nubile girls dancing naked all over the place, and what was really funny was that on the wall they were showing pornographic movies. Now, I've seen a little bit of soft porn, Candy Barr and stuff like that, but this was the real thing and I have to tell you, watching the walls with Rose Marie covering my eyes was not easy. Lily was so disgusted with the display that she got up and left immediately.

The rest of us had a drink, but everybody was pretty uncomfortable, so we got out of there after about twenty minutes. Shortly after we left, the place was raided and everyone went to jail, including the customers. It was a huge thing in the newspapers the next day. And I have to tell you, I wish we hadn't left. Just to see Paul Lynde behind bars for going to a topless bar would have been worth a lot of money to me.

Of course, we all went to a lot of parties together. I remember the year that Karen Valentine had just moved into a beautiful home in Sherman Oaks and was having her first party. She had invited all her friends from *Room 222* and *The Hollywood Squares*. Well, the party was supposed to begin at 7:30 and

John Byner on *The Peter Marshall Variety Show*, probably doing the same routine he did to cheer Karen Valentine up at her party.

147

at 7:30 no one was there except John Byner. Since it was the first big party she'd ever given, Karen immediately assumed nobody was going to show up. She got so upset that John, trying to cheer her up, started doing impressions of everyone who was invited until the guests finally started to arrive.

That was the night Paul was so unhappy because Karen was seriously dating Jon Hager of the Hager twins, a country western singing act of the seventies. We were in Karen's bedroom and Paul, who was dead drunk, said, "She can't marry him. He's not good enough for her," then fell down and hit his head on the doorjamb so hard we actually thought he was dead and called the paramedics.

Paul didn't give a lot of parties and I rarely saw him socially except at events that had to do with the show. But he had just moved into a home off Doheny and Sunset that had once belonged to Errol Flynn, and he decided to have a dinner party to show it off. He invited quite a few people from the

Bernadette Peters was so cute and feminine.
No wonder Steve Martin fell for her.

Roger Moore, Judy Carne, yours truly, and Douglas Fairbanks Jr. Judy's sweet face belied a mouth a New York cabbie would be proud of.

show and I was one of them. It just so happened that Bob Newhart's opening act in Vegas canceled and I was asked to fill in, for a lot of money, I might add. I called Paul and told him I wouldn't be able to make it and why. He couldn't believe it. I was actually giving up an evening at his home in favor of working. Especially since, and this was the first I'd heard about it, he was giving the party just for me.

"C'mon, Paul," I said. "You're not giving this party for me. You're giving it for you." The next time I saw Paul, he didn't seem angry, but that was the last time I was ever invited to his home.

Quite a few romances started on *The Hollywood Squares* and they were always so much fun to watch. One night we had Steve Martin and Bernadette Peters on the show. You couldn't miss the attraction between them. By the dinner break, you would have thought they were on their first date. While they never married, their relationship lasted quite a while.

And sometimes we had just the opposite of romance. Like the time we had booked Judy Carne for the first three shows of a nighttime taping and Burt Reynolds for the second three shows. As luck would have it, he came a little early, she left a little late, and they ran into each other on the set. They were going through a messy divorce at the time and Judy was never one to hold her tongue very well, so we were all treated to a few well-placed expletives that night.

Shirley Jones did the show with Marty Ingels years before they ever got together, but I like to think it might have been the start of their friendship.

My favorite romance is the one between Tom Poston and Suzanne Pleshette—not that they met on *Hollywood Squares*. They were actually on Broadway together when she was just a youngster, and years afterwards they both worked on *The Bob Newhart Show.* For many years, Suzanne and Tom were each happily married, Suzanne to Tommy Gallagher and Tom to Kay Hudson Poston. Tom and Kay were Laurie's and my closest friends. Even though Kay suffered from ALS, Lou Gehrig's disease, she managed to

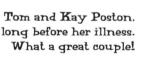

Tom and Kay Poston,
long before her illness.
What a great couple!

TOM POSTON
SUZANNE PLESHETTE

ORIGINAL BROADWAY PRODUCTION

ORIGINAL CAST REVIVAL

NEW YORK LIMITED RUN

LOS ANGELES UNLIMITED RUN

"The maturity they bring to their roles adds a richness that was missing in their original run. It's the gift of time and experience, and one can clearly see they're having a ball!"

SPECIAL HOLIDAY AND NEW YEAR APPEARANCES.
2000   2001

Tom and Suzanne's Christmas card says it all.

keep our social lives organized. She was the one who always got the theater tickets, made the dinner reservations, and told everybody what to bring to the picnic. She died on July 10, 1998, and left a tremendous void. Tom was just heartsick; it made me so sad to feel his pain.

Tommy Gallagher also suffered from a long illness and died about the same time as Kay, leaving Suzanne devastated. Tom and Suzanne may have started seeing each other out of mutual grief, but they fell madly in love and in a few short months were married in New York City, where they first met. This was followed by a gala Hollywood reception with four or five hundred of their closest friends in attendance.

And there were some romances in the office. Quite a few, as a matter of fact. I told you that Merrill Heatter and Bob Quigley were fair and wonderful employers and their employees returned their loyalty, but Merrill and Bob did have a few rules. Quig didn't like women to wear pants. I don't know if it was because he was an old-fashioned guy, or if it was because he loved to see the female members of the staff in the micro-mini skirts of the day, but it was a quirk most of the women didn't mind going along with. Everybody was crazy about Quig.

Another thing they asked from their staff was that they not date each other. This wasn't written down anywhere; it was just something everybody knew. And the employees took this edict so seriously that before *The Hollywood Squares* had celebrated its fifth anniversary, there had been three inter-office weddings. First, Hope Berg and Warren Murray. Hope was one of the first H-Q people I met and Warren was the son of comedian Jan Murray. Warren came to work for Heatter/Quigley as a writer for a game

Warren and Hope Murray, twenty years after they were married, three years before they were divorced.

Bill and Adrienne Armstrong lighting a candle at the bar mitzvah of Jack Carter's son, Michael.

show called *Funny You Should Ask.* The two of them shared an office and before you knew it, they were sharing their lives.

Next was Bill Armstrong and Adrienne Rhoden. He was the producer of the show and she was the production secretary. He lived in North Hollywood, and she lived in Sherman Oaks. The next thing we knew, they both were living in Encino as husband and wife.

Then came Randy Freer and Susie Rockett. He was the stepson of Art Alisi and she was the beautiful, blond daughter of a well known set designer. They both worked as production assistants on various Heatter/Quigley shows and had a gorgeous wedding that we all attended one glorious Sunday afternoon.

It just goes to show, in affairs of the heart, you can't dictate who will be attracted to whom, and many marriages are, after all, made in the workplace. I have to give this to Merrill and Bob, though. All three of those marriages did end in divorce, so I guess they might have been right.

One of the guys on our show was well known as a ladies' man. He couldn't resist hitting on every good-looking woman who showed up, including staff members, contestants, and stars. You know that old saying, "If you throw enough stuff against the wall, some of it is bound to stick"? I guess it's true, because this man got lucky more often than anybody I've ever known.

One time a beautiful black actress was on the panel. I'm not going to name names, but she had a series at the time that was quite hot. Mr. Lucky

Randy Freer
and Susie
Rockett on their
wedding day.

became very chummy with her during dinner and when the taping was over, they left together. Turns out, Mrs. Lucky was out of town visiting her parents, and the beautiful actress ended up spending the night at his house. As she was leaving in the morning, a neighbor was standing on the sidewalk. Mr. Lucky was noticeably flustered.

"Don't worry about a thing," said the actress. She quickly tied her scarf around her head, picked up a mop and a bucket, and headed toward her car. Never missing a beat, Mr. Lucky called after her.

"Next time, don't forget the Ajax."

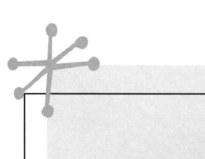

13

The Contestants

Many of the people who were contestants on our show will surprise you.

tars were certainly a big part of our show, probably the most important element, but other people also helped make our show what it was. I'm talking about the contestants. We were very fussy about the contestants we used, so we had to see lots of them in order to pick the cream of the crop. I'm pretty sure we were the only show to interview everyone from the studio audience. After a taping, we would invite those who were interested in being a contestant to stay. We'd ask them at least three questions, and those who showed promise were asked to climb into a square on the set and stand in for one of our stars. That way, we were pretty sure we had contestants who not only could talk, but looked good on camera as well.

Once in a while, we'd find somebody in the studio audience from out of town who was so cute we'd push him or her right up onto the show. Now our contestants had to bring changes of clothes, just like the stars did, in case they stayed on for more than one day. The out-of-town contestants never had a change of clothes with them, so we'd have to scurry around looking for something for them to wear. To alleviate this problem, Ida Mae started collecting all kinds of colorful scarves. If you ever saw a contestant draped in a scarf on their second day on the show, you'd know they were one of our last-minute discoveries.

In all the years of doing *Squares,* I only had to stop tapings a couple of times because the contestant turned out to be someone I knew. They would never tell, of course, because they wanted to be on the show, so if a contestant looked even vaguely familiar to me, I'd stop the tape and be sure I didn't know them personally. This didn't make me too popular with neighbors, my dry cleaner, or the parents of my children's friends, but Compliance and Practices, the NBC legal department, was very strict, and I couldn't take a chance of jeopardizing the show.

I think the biggest faux pas I ever made on the show was with a contestant. He was a postal worker and I don't know what I was thinking, but when he lost and I was saying good-bye I said, "Well, you've won $600 and that's pretty good for a mailman." Sometimes I marvel at my own insensitivity.

I wasn't the only one who made an occasional blunder. When Susan St. James was on the show, Art Alisi kept trying to put her in the contestant room. He just couldn't seem to get it through his head that she was one of the stars.

Don Rickles didn't mind being offensive to contestants. It fit right into his act. I remember a contestant whose name was Joe Louis, and Don did a good two minutes on the name. "Joe, you've changed," he said, because this contestant was white. Then I announced that this Joe Louis was a black-belt karate instructor, and Don, feigning fright, said, "No offense, Joe. You want to spit on my suit?"

Sometimes I would get these vibes from women contestants, like maybe they were interested in me. You know, little things, like they'd take my hand and put it on their leg during a commercial. But I'm proud to say I never succumbed to that temptation, even when I was single. The good news is that years later, occasionally I would run into these lovely women again with no reason whatsoever not to pursue their friendship—so I did.

And speaking of attractive female contestants, we once had one who gave her occupation as a recreational therapist. During the break between shows, Pat Buttram, who played Mr. Haney on *Green Acres* and *Petticoat Junction,* told me he was surprised to see her there, because she was actually a call girl whose services he had once used. We decided it was best to just keep it quiet and let the game go on.

We once had a lucky contestant who won a car in the secret square. Of course, the contestants didn't actually get the car that night, but to make it look authentic, I asked if someone had a set of keys I could hand him on camera. Art Alisi threw me some car keys that were lying around and I presented them to the contestant. Hours later we discovered that I'd given him the keys to one of our producers' cars and the contestant had driven it home.

Sometimes we had special contestants, celebrities in their own right. One

One of
our lovely
Rose Queen
contestants.

year we had beauty queens who had held the title Miss Gazzarri A-Go-Go, and one of them was Catherine Bach. Also, Mary Fitzgerald, a former Miss Teen America, later won more than $10,000 in cash and prizes on our show. Rona Barrett, who became a famous gossip columnist, was a contestant on *People Will Talk,* and then did run-throughs for *The Hollywood Squares* as a contestant. She later appeared on the show as one of the stars. And a yearly tradition that I always enjoyed was having the lovely Rose Bowl Queen as a contestant.

Naomi Judd was once a contestant. Jay Redack ran into her recently and she told him that the money she won on the show literally saved her life. She was on welfare at the time, a single mom trying to support her two little girls, Ashley and Wynonna.

Our contestant coordinators also liked to have fun, so they would try to find contestants who resembled the stars. One night we had a JoAnne Worley look-alike who was pretty good, but the capper came when somebody found a guy who looked almost exactly like Wally. I mean, it was uncanny. I couldn't even look at the contestant without bursting into laughter, and of course, he called on Wally at every opportunity. I may not have had the presence of mind to ask for photos with Gloria Swanson or Helen Hayes, but I couldn't resist getting one with this Wally look-alike.

O. J. Simpson was a great college football player, winner of the Heisman Trophy, and he wanted to be a contestant. It wasn't that he loved the show so much, but that he really needed the money. Since he'd never even seen

Will the real Wally please stand up? Oh, they are standing up.

the show, Art Alisi suggested he watch a taping or two before going on. He sat with Ida Mae McKenzie, who tried to point out how the game was played. After one show, O. J. was champing at the bit. "I'm ready, Mama," he told Ida Mae. Well, we put him on the show and he did okay. He won a few hundred dollars. When he was finished, he went to Ida Mae.

"Where do I go to get my money?" he asked.

"You'll have to wait for it to be mailed to you," Ida Mae explained.

A very disappointed O. J. left the studio that night. Years later, O. J. came back as the only contestant ever to return as a star on the show.

And speaking of stars, *The Hollywood Squares* always supported the Vince Lombardi celebrity golf tournament in Menomonee Falls, Wisconsin. Bart Starr, famous quarterback and coach of the Green Bay Packers, and his wife, Cherry, hosted an annual cocktail party at the Beverly Hills Hotel to invite celebrities to participate in the tournament. One year I was chatting with Cherry, who was a lovely lady, and she said to me, "Pete, I love your show. I'd really like to be on it."

"I'm sure we can work that out," I told her. "When would you like to do it?"

"Oh, as soon as I can," she said, starting to get excited.

I was already figuring out how we could get a famous female athlete's husband to play Mr. X to Cherry Starr's circle and they could play for their favorite charity—it would be a great promotion for the golf tournament and a chance to do something charitable on the show.

Just then, Bart wandered over. I slapped him on the back and said, "I just told Cherry I can get her on the show as a contestant."

Cherry's face fell. "A contestant? Oh, no. I wanted to be in one of those little boxes." Luckily, Bart deflected Cherry's attention to some visitors she had to greet and I was off the hook.

Being a huge baseball fan, I'll never forget when Dick Williams was a contestant. He had just taken over as manager of the Boston Red Sox and I was really hoping he'd win a lot of money, but he lost rather quickly. Then we found out we had made a mistake and he had actually been correct on the question he'd lost on. He was the first contestant we ever brought back because of that kind of error on the show. On his return, he earned $50,000, the most money ever won by a contestant to date. I told him right then that

Wally, Cliff, Mamie Van Doren, Mickey Callan, Rose Marie, a very happy Dick Williams, Barbara Feldon, Noel Harrison, me, Paul, and Abby.

he was on a roll and was going to win the pennant. I wish I'd gone to Vegas and made that bet, because sure enough the Sox did win and I've got to tell you, nobody expected it that year, least of all Dick.

I think the sponsor that became most associated with the show over the years was Dicker & Dicker of Beverly Hills. Some lucky contestants won luxurious fur coats that they could actually wear in those days. We used to have one of the female stars model the furs and it was always a lot of fun. One night, the star who was supposed to be the model decided she should get paid extra for that chore, so at the last minute I put on the fur and modeled it myself.

Dicker & Dicker was actually a wholesaler of furs and didn't have a retail establishment when they first started with *The Hollywood Squares*. Then tourists started pouring in to Beverly Hills looking for the famous furrier. They finally had to open a store in Century City and almost every day you could find hordes of tourists taking pictures in front of it.

As I mentioned, a lot was always going on at NBC at the time of *The Hollywood Squares*, and sometimes wonderful stars would be sharing our makeup room or just wandering around in the halls. Once in a while, they'd surprise us with unexpected appearances, like the time Chevy Chase did a crawl-on. Occasionally, Art Alisi would talk a visiting celebrity into coming on the show as a make-believe contestant. When a real contestant would lose and we'd cut to a commercial, we'd bring out one of these stars in the contestant's seat. We'd come back on-camera and there would be Jack Benny or Bob Hope. Once we had two surprise contestants, Dudley Moore and Susan Anton. After we introduced them and enjoyed the joke, they would leave. But when we ran into Jerry Lewis and he agreed to sit in as a contestant, he actually insisted on playing the game. He donated the money and prizes he won to Muscular Dystrophy.

Another important element of the show was the live audience. You don't think too much about them, but without their presence and their reactions, the panel wouldn't have anybody to play to, and the show would lose so much. Because of this, we hired audience bookers to be sure we always had a full house, and we tried to keep a fast pace going so they wouldn't get bored.

One night a technical snafu forced taping to stop for about half an hour.

Larry Storch, the brilliant nightclub comedian and one of the stars of the 1960s comedy *F Troop*, volunteered to keep the audience interested, and proceeded to do his nightclub act for the studio crowd. At one point he was doing funny translations from French to English and one of them was "Honoré de Balzac. No hitting below the belt." Part of our bused-in audience that night was a group of Catholic high school girls and on that particular line one of the nuns stood up, clapped her hands, and said, "Come along, girls!" and led them all out.

And on one famous evening nobody was getting laughs, not even Paul, and we later discovered the audience booker had brought us two busloads of deaf people who couldn't speak, let alone laugh out loud.

I once duped a few members of our audience, but it was in a very good cause. Our producer, Bill Armstrong, had a wonderful dog named Sam, who had just given birth to her first litter of puppies. Now, if you don't think there's such a thing as an ugly puppy, you never saw this litter. Bill was having a terrible time finding homes for these dogs—and I do mean dogs. Out of sheer desperation, Bill brought the pups to a taping, hoping some kind-hearted soul on the show might want one. No luck. That's when I got my inspiration. It was the early show and quite a few youngsters were in the audience, so I went out during the warm-up with the dogs in a cute little basket. I told the audience my dog had just given birth and I was looking for good homes for my puppies. I saw kids turn to their parents with pleading eyes and before I knew it, a slew of kids were clamoring to take these poor pups home. We gave them to the ones whose parents were in attendance and agreed it was okay, and never heard from them again. That was thirty years ago and those dogs are long gone, but I know they had wonderful lives with the families that adopted them—and I'm sure they turned into great pets, just like their mother.

I didn't get out of this escapade unscathed, by the way. Earl Holliman, a very active member of Actors and Others for Animals was on the show that night and he issued me a stern warning never to do something like that again. He was rightfully concerned about what kind of homes the dogs would end up in.

After that, we started a program with Actors and Others for Animals to try to place homeless dogs in good homes. We used to bring the animals out during the break, introduce them to the audience, and if someone fell in love with a dog, an AOA member would visit to see if they and the animal were right for each other. I'm proud to say my little deception ended up making a lot of puppies and people a little happier.

One night our audience got a special treat when I ran into Jimmy Durante in the hallway between shows and asked him to do a walk-on. So when Kenny Williams said, "And here is the Master of *The Hollywood Squares*, Peter Marshall," Jimmy walked out instead of me. Steve Allen was on the panel that night, and without a pause he said, "Hey, Peter, that's great! Now do Bogart."

14

Some Traveling Music, Please

Our trips to Puerto Vallarta,
Vancouver, Jamaica, and Bakersfield.

O ne of the best things about having a show like *The Hollywood Squares* was the trips we'd go on. They were usually publicity junkets, plugging "Beautiful British Columbia Week" or something like that. Anyway, everything was paid for and we were encouraged to bring along as many stars as we wanted, so as you can imagine, these were usually the most fun trips in the world.

We went to Puerto Vallarta, and we actually had the whole plane to ourselves, except for two rows in first class. As we boarded the plane, we saw three people in those two rows, a nurse, a companion, and Richard Burton. Apparently, he was on a trip to his home in Puerto Vallarta (without Elizabeth) to dry out. He watched us board as if he were thinking, who are these people invading my plane? A lot of well-known folks were on that trip, among them Michele Lee and Jimmy Farentino, Karen Valentine and Jon Hager, and Rob Reiner and Penny Marshall (who made the mistake of eating chocolate-covered strawberries at the airport, got deathly ill, and spent the rest of the trip in their rooms). But when Vincent Price and Coral Browne boarded the plane at the end, Burton lit up. They knew each other quite well. Of course, Vinnie and Coral seemed to know everybody. He used to say things like, "I'm going to London to see Larry and Vivian, and spend a little time with Alec"—meaning Laurence Olivier, Vivian Leigh, and Alec Guinness.

At one point, Karen Valentine got up to go to the bathroom and passed Burton. They exchanged greetings. She was very impressed. So was he.

The next day, Karen happened to pass Coral on the beach. Coral took fifteen minutes of sun every day, no more and no less. When Coral saw Karen, she stopped her. "Oh, Karen. Little Dickie Burton called—well, he actually didn't call—he sent a message by burro. He wants to know if you'll come to dinner tomorrow." Well, you didn't have to ask Karen twice. This was Richard Burton, after all. It happened to be Vinnie's birthday and the day before Karen's birthday, so Burton decided to have a party to celebrate both events. Everybody was invited, and it soon became clear that what Richard Burton was really interested in was a little time alone with Karen. Well, he never got it and he became more and more morose. At one point Karen looked at him and said, "Don't you ever smile?" But it was fun watching the great English actor mooning over the young teacher from *Room 222*.

■ ■ ■

On a promotional trip to Vancouver, British Columbia, Rose Marie, the easiest person in the world to get along with, got it into her head that the Canadians were looking down on her. Immediately, everything they did irritated her. She felt like she was being treated as the ugly American for no reason. When they asked her to sign autographs, she thought they were being condescending. I never saw Ro get so bristly. A couple of nights into the trip, we were at a lovely dinner and Ro was still grousing around about Canadians with their noses in the air. As they served the bouillon, I told her it was time to get over it.

"Okay," said Ro. "Watch this." She looked up at her waiter. "Excuse me. I see you're serving bouillon, but you seem to have forgotten the bouillon spoon."

The waiter pointed out her soupspoon. "Oh, no," said Ro. "That's a soupspoon. Much too large for bouillon, you know."

Well, this poor waiter asked the maitre d', who went into the kitchen and had a meeting with the chef before coming back to our table empty-handed. "I'm sorry," he said to Ro. "We don't seem to have any bouillon spoons in the restaurant, but you can rest assured there will be some here tomorrow."

"Thank you very much," said Ro, in a grand lady voice. "I guess this will have to do for now." And she proceeded to eat her soup.

When the maitre d' left I asked her, "Ro, what the hell is a bouillon spoon?"

"Damned if I know," said Ro, "but I feel a lot better now." Ro was her usual self for the rest of the trip.

Later, a high tea was given for us at the beautiful Empress Hotel in Victoria. It was four in the afternoon and the sun filtered through the trees and into the gorgeous outdoor atrium where the tea was being held. Karen Valentine and JoAnne Worley had spent some time putting on their makeup, deciding what they were going to wear, and getting their hair just right. The two women were busy complimenting each other on how good they looked, when Paul Lynde swished in sporting a great tan and a Greta Garbo hat. He examined their faces closely and said, "You girls should never come outside at this time of day." They both laughed, but I could see he'd taken some of the wind out of their sails.

■ ■ ■

Now let me tell you about our Christmas trip to Jamaica, circa 1976. Maybe the moon was in the wrong place, but almost every couple on that trip barely made it through still speaking to each other. We left on the day after Christmas and the trip lasted through the New Year. We flew into Kingston and had a two-hour bus trip along a winding, zigzag road to Montego Bay.

That's Art Alisi in the buffet line with Rue McClanahan, on our Christmas trip to Jamaica. For some reason, I don't think that's milk everyone is drinking.

George cutting into a coconut. It's a miracle he didn't cut his hand off.

About halfway there, Marcia Wallace, who suffers from car sickness, began to throw up. We stopped the bus and everybody got off for a breath of fresh air. That's when Karen Valentine, who was reading the itinerary, noticed we were scheduled for another two-hour bus trip back to Kingston the next day for a luncheon with the governor. Well, we still had another hour left to go on this trip and nobody was having a very good time, so Karen suggested they bring the governor to us. That idea didn't fly, but they did assure us they had planes available so we wouldn't have to take another bus ride.

I was told going to the Palace to meet the governor was a very political thing, and you had to be careful to follow the customs and not offend anyone. Since I would be seated on the dais with the governor, and Sally and I weren't married yet, I suggested it might be better if she didn't sit with me on the dais. This might not have been the most diplomatic thing I've ever done. She got so mad, she refused to go to the luncheon at all.

I left her at the hotel and a bunch of us got on a decent-sized private plane, bound for Kingston. Everyone was there, except Karen Valentine and her fiancé, Gary Verna. (Incidentally, Karen and Gary were married one year later in Reno and just celebrated their twenty-fourth wedding anniversary, but back to Jamaica.) When they finally showed up, Karen actually looked relieved to learn the plane was full. Turns out she was deathly afraid of small planes. She and Gary headed back to the car, all smiles, when a really tiny plane pulled up to take the late arrivals. With no way out, Karen and Gary boarded the little crop duster. Paul, being the good friend he was, decided to fly with them.

Our plane arrived with no problems, except for Marcia's second bout with travel sickness, and we all watched as the smaller plane made its bumpy landing. I'm still not sure how the pilot was able to land the plane at all, since Paul had his arms wound tightly around his neck and was yelling "We're gonna die" in his ear for the whole trip. When they disembarked, Karen and Gary were a little wobbly, but Paul actually got down and kissed the ground.

We were taken directly to the Governor's Palace for press interviews. A reporter asked Paul what his favorite Christmas carol was and he sang out "Fall on Your Knees" in his best Paul Lynde voice. We screamed. Karen was mortified. "Paul, you can't say that in the Palace." But of course, Paul could and did say just about anything he wanted to, which really made this trip fun, in spite of the strange happenings between some of the couples.

Now it was time for the luncheon. I was seated on one side of the governor, and I think the seat on the other side must have been reserved for Sally, because suddenly, the governor's assistant was looking for a single woman to seat there. Somebody grabbed Rose Marie and plunked her down next to the governor. Apparently, he felt very insecure about entertaining a bunch of Americans and started asking her what he was supposed to do. Should he introduce people in any special order? Should he make his speech before dessert or after? Ro did her best with the answers, and the next thing she knew she was in the reception line with the governor, greeting people. She was doing fine until Paul came through the line. "Nice to see you," he said. "I love your house." That's when she lost it.

By the time I got back from the luncheon, Sally, who was still furious, had arranged for a private plane to fly her back to Kingston. In retrospect, it might have been better for both of us if she had gone.

Marcia had brought a guy she'd been seeing for quite some time and she hoped this trip would be the catalyst for the relationship to become more intimate. After the luncheon and her second round of upchucking, they had a little talk.

"Do you ever find that the more you like someone, the less you want to sleep with them?" he asked her.

"You couldn't tell me that in Van Nuys?" responded Marcia.

Marcia Wallace and friends, enjoying the New Year's Eve party.

Hi, I'm
your
bunny,
Peter.

Paul had also brought a date he was very excited about—a really hot young guy who suddenly felt it wasn't fair not to disclose the fact that he had a slight case of VD.

"You couldn't tell me that in Van Nuys?" responded Paul.

Leslie Uggams and Grahame Pratt got into a huge fight and he locked her out of the room. Their long marriage was put to the test on this trip. Happily, it survived.

As I recall, Alex Trebek was being touted as one of Lin Bolen's hot new glamour boys, and she had urged him not to flaunt the fact that he was married. This did not sit well with his wife, Elaine, and caused more than a few words between them.

The only couples that never had any problems at all were Jonathan Winters and his wife, Rue McClanahan and Gus (it was their honeymoon), and my sister Joanne and her husband, C. V. Wood, who absolutely adored her and never got mad at her for anything.

On New Year's Eve, Paul invited Karen and Gary to his room for a drink. He wanted to be sure he and Karen weren't wearing the same gown. Paul was wearing a caftan, lots of gold jewelry, and sandals. On the way to the party, they ran into Jonathan Winters, who was dressed as a yacht captain. He took one look at Paul and quipped, "Obviously, you're from the Holy Land."

During that trip, it seemed like we were forever standing in lines. I used to try to get near Paul and Jonathan because they were constantly fooling around and it was always good for a laugh. One day we were waiting in line for something or other, and Paul and Jonathan were passing the time by pantomiming a grenade toss. It got more and more outrageous as they tried to keep the grenade from hitting the ground. Poor Art Fleming, the original host of *Jeopardy!*, unknowingly stepped between them and detonated the grenade, putting a fast end to the fun. Art, whose sense of humor didn't quite match up with the others, never could figure out why Paul and Jonathan were so upset.

■ ■ ■

When the Vince Lombardi Celebrity Golf Tournament began in Menomonee Falls, Wisconsin, the organizers called Bill Armstrong to see if we could bring some folks from the show to participate. Needless to say, we were all happy to do so. Most everybody went in couples, but one year McLean Stevenson was alone. He struck up a friendship with a flight attendant on our plane, and the next thing we knew, she was staying with him at our hotel.

There was a big party and Sally and I stayed late, along with Bill and Adrienne. The four of us were heading back to our room, when we passed what we thought was McLean's room and the door was slightly ajar. We'd all been doing a pretty good job of partying and we decided nothing would be funnier than to burst in on McLean and serenade him and his new lady friend.

We pushed open the door and sneaked in, and by the light of the window saw that it wasn't McLean at all. Instead, we'd walked in on Cameron Mitchell and his new wife, Margaret, the very proper widow of a Southern senator. We were shocked and they were stunned. We sort of nodded, turned, and surreptitiously left the room. Hopefully, they continued.

■ ■ ■

This wasn't really a *Hollywood Squares* trip, but it involved some of our people. Nanette's husband had written a script that was going to be shot in Italy during a summer hiatus, which Nanette was starring in. She felt since they were going to be on location for six weeks, it would be great to have people she liked with her, so they hired Abby Dalton and Wally Cox to be in the film. One afternoon they were having lunch and Wally ordered something he'd never had before—pigeon. Well, the waiter brought it on a silver dish under glass, and when he whipped off the top with a "voila," the bird was still wearing its head. Wally was not a vegetarian by any means, but he loved birds in their natural state and this one came a little too close to that for comfort. He went absolutely pale, took his napkin off his lap, and covered the bird with it. The waiter was horrified and had a meeting with the chef. Soon everybody came out of the kitchen and stood around the table, demanding to know what the problem was. Wally was so upset he couldn't even speak. He left the restaurant without a word, leaving a bunch of Italians scratching their heads and shrugging their shoulders over the erratic behavior of the little American.

During the filming, the leading man developed a crush on Abby. The star of the film was Susan St. James, and even though she was completely uninterested in the actor, her nose got a little out of joint because he was infatuated by Abby instead of her. This led to some discomfort between the two actresses, but Abby thoroughly enjoyed the few weeks of flattering attention.

The one thing this trip brought into clear focus was Nanette's unerringly optimistic nature and her ability to look at things in the best light. One day, she and Abby were standing in line, waiting their turns to use a bathroom that didn't even have a toilet in it. Everything around them was totally filthy and Abby was really missing the comforts of home. Out of nowhere, Nanette said, "Look, Abby, isn't it wonderful?"

"Isn't what wonderful?"

Nanette smiled and pointed out a dusty window. "The way the sun glistens off the pigeon droppings."

■ ■ ■

My brother, David, talked me into investing in a discotheque in Bakersfield, California, called The Yum Yum Room. I rented a bus, filled it with booze, and invited everybody from *Squares* and some other friends of mine to be my guests at the grand opening. Fifty of us took this terrible trip up Interstate 5 to Bakersfield. Dennis James's brother, Mike Sposa, got so drunk that he ended up passing out for the rest of the night, and never got off the bus—which turned out to be the smartest move anybody could have made.

When we got there, the place was jammed and I started seeing dollar signs. Inside, members of the press were waiting for us to do interviews, but it was so noisy we couldn't hear a thing. Terrible heavy-metal music was blaring and young kids were dancing, but I don't think anybody was buying drinks but me. After about an hour, we left, and by that time everybody was so depressed that whoever wasn't already snockered got that way on the bus. Then we slept all the way back to NBC. Incidentally, I never saw a penny of my money back on that investment.

■ ■ ■

Now I know an earthquake isn't a trip, but I wanted to mention it and, for some reason, this seemed like the logical place to me. We were taping when the first big aftershock from the earthquake of 1971 hit. To tell you the truth, the whole experience is kind of a blur, but I do remember Paul, who had been dieting for a month, running to the candy machine and buying one of each. We also lost a young cameraman to the earthquake. Oh, he didn't die or anything. He simply leapt from the platform, ran out of the studio, and was never heard from again—sort of like my discotheque.

Wally, me, Dennis James, Sid Melton, Rose Marie, and Tom Kennedy (in back) ready to have some fun in Bakersfield. Wrong!

15

Letters, We Get Letters

Outrageous and outraged letters received by the show over the years, including one from an incensed John Wayne.

can't even begin to estimate how many letters we received over the course of the show's run. Most of them were sent to the office, and it's anybody's guess what happened to them from there. Bill Armstrong used to save a few and bring them to parties to read. Like the one that said simply, "Dear Mr. Marshall, Please send me something." Of course, I didn't. It would have been an impossible task to answer all the letters that came our way.

Many times I received gifts, such as homemade cookies and embroidered T-shirts with my name on them, but I don't have any of those mementos either. NBC never allowed us to keep anything that came unsolicited in the mail.

But I do remember a few letters that told of how our show actually made an important difference in people's lives. Like the family who suddenly found themselves in the middle of a tornado. A recent question on the show had been, "Where is the safest place to be during a tornado?" and the answer was, "If you don't have a basement, get into the bathtub." Well, this family of four remembered seeing that show and followed our advice. They sent a picture of the whole family huddled together in a small tub and that was the only thing left standing. Their entire house had been blown away. They credited *The Hollywood Squares* with saving their lives.

Another man had been watching the show when this question was asked: "What should you do if your television set catches on fire? Should you turn it off, throw water on it, or run immediately out of the house?" The answer was, "Run immediately out of the house." That's exactly what this man did, and he escaped serious injury when the set blew up and caused a fire that destroyed his home.

One unsigned letter said, "I think Hollywood Squies is too mixed up with to many interreptions by the pannell." From that time on, Bill and Les always referred to the show as "Squies" and never called the group of stars anything but "the pannell."

Some of the other viewer mail was equally weird. Charley Weaver often used the name of the actor Efrem Zimbalist Jr. as a joke answer. For example, I'd ask the question, "Charley, what do you call that thing in your throat that quivers when you sing?" He'd answer, "Efrem Zimbalist Jr." We thought it was a funny running gag. A woman wrote a letter accusing Cliff of being in the employ of the Communists or the Mafia and trying to discredit the FBI. At the time, *The FBI* was a popular television series starring none other than Efrem Zimbalist Jr.

Eartha Kitt wasn't on the show that often, but one time she created quite a stir and generated a ton of mail and my first death threat. She had gone to a White House luncheon—some affair honoring women—and berated Lady Bird Johnson about the Vietnam War, almost making the First Lady cry. We had taped the show several weeks earlier, but her shows aired the week after this incident and NBC was deluged with angry letters and phone calls, and I got quite a few myself. One of them was from an irate viewer from Texas. He said he had a gun and he was coming to L.A. to kill me. Now, let me tell you how bright this person was. He wrote his return address on the envelope. I passed the letter along to somebody at the network, and before I knew it, the FBI was involved. I don't know what happened, but I do remember being told I had nothing to worry about any longer.

We received a very nice letter from Ann Landers, whose column we used as a great source of material.

Ann Landers
Publishers - Hall Syndicate
Chicago Sun-Times - Daily News Building
Chicago, Illinois 60611

December 27, 1974

Peter Marshall
Hollywood Squares
NBC
3000 West Alameda Plaza
Burbank, California 91523

Dear Peter:

I love Hollywood Squares. But then -- doesn't everybody?

I see the program often and it is one of the freshest, liveliest afloat. Everywhere I go someone says, "They used an Ann Landers question on Hollywood Squares today and it was great."

Well, today you used TWO questions involving Ann Landers. Arty Johnson's answer to "Can a couple have a successful marriage with very little sex?" was a scream. You will recall that he responded, "It depends on who is getting very little."

Then the second question was put to Rosemarie -- "Can you tell the kind of life a woman has lived by looking at her face?" Her answer was a gasser. She replied, "You can tell the kind of life Ann Landers leads by looking at HER face -- but not mine!"

Please give them each a gold star and a big kiss for me. And have one yourself.

Consider this letter a personal invitation to call me when you next come to Chicago. My unlisted home phone number is 787-1234. Please have the number tatooed on your hip and eat this letter. The number is very private.

My best wishes for a healthy, happy, productive New Year.

Sincerely,

AL:ms

We also received a lovely thank you letter from Henry Fonda, which I still have in my collection.

HENRY FONDA

May 20, 1976

Dear Peter and All My Friends at
    Hollywood Squares,

    I am sorry I am having to dictate this,
but my right arm is still not steady enough
and strong enough yet, and I can't put off
any longer thanking you all for the terrarium
which has happily joined my collection.

    I really appreciate your good thoughts
and send you all of my very best.

Hank

Of course, the letter I prize the most is hanging in my den, and I'm so grateful to Gary Johnson for seeing that I got it. It was in response to this question on the show: "According to Rona Barrett, what do John Wayne's children call him?" The joke was: "Sir."

Here's the letter I received from the Duke himself, John Wayne.

This picture, along with the letter, hangs on the wall in my den.

J O H N   W A Y N E

9570 Wilshire Blvd., Suite 400
Beverly Hills, California 90212
April 14, 1975

Mr. Peter Marshall
c/o The Hollywood Squares
NBC
3000 West Alameda
Burbank, California

Dear Mr. Marshall:

I take a dim view of your assumptions concerning my life
and my family. My children are the dearest things in my
life, and I speak to them with nothing but affection; and I
God damned well resent your saying that I make them call
me Sir, and I suggest that you correct it on your show or
don't ever pass me on the street.

I am available. I have an office with two secretaries. It is
mighty easy to check the verity of your trivia. Please don't
misunderstand me. I mean this.

Sincerely,

John Wayne

John Wayne

JW/ps

Here are just a few of the wonderful people who made *The Hollywood Squares* the great show that it was.

16

It Couldn't Last Forever

When and how the show finally got canceled.

I knew that *Squares* was ending when Lin Bolen came to NBC with all these new ideas. Her concept of a good show was a show with a great set and an emcee in an open shirt.

I remember Lin's first production, *The Wizard of Odds*. For its time, it was the most innovative set I ever saw in my life, all depending on electronics and lights before computers made that so easy to do. As a result, the set was constantly breaking down and the game was the worst. Lin gave the show to a bright new guy from Canada by the name of Alex Trebek. To give you some idea of how smart Alex is (or how *not* smart the rest of us were), he's the only game show host I've ever seen work without cue cards.

Alex Trebek and me guesting on *The Magnificent Marble Machine* and sporting the new Lin Bolen look.

Lin disrupted everything at NBC. She took off the best hour we had—from 11:00 A.M. to noon was *Jeopardy!*, followed by *Squares,* and we kicked butt with that hour of television. She decided to cancel *Jeopardy!*, which was the best lead-in in the world. Merv Griffin, who owned the show, had a contract with NBC, so to appease him, Lin gave him a pilot deal for a little show called *Wheel of Fortune.* I was at the taping of that pilot, which was originally named *Shopper's Bazaar* and starred Ed "Kookie" Byrnes from *77 Sunset Strip.* I was blown away by the set, which looked like a French country museum. Doesn't sound familiar? That's because it's not the set they ended up using, but it was gorgeous.

Marty Pasetta, the director of that pilot, came up with an overhead shot of the wheel that was a stroke of genius. In fact, they still use that shot today, and Marty gets paid every time they do, and deservedly so.

Nobody was too excited about the pilot. First of all, it broke all the game show rules. At that time, network executives believed that a game show shouldn't have to be watched, but could just be listened to. This was so housewives could listen to the television without affecting their ironing or other chores. Thankfully, times have changed since then.

In the beginning, the show didn't really do any numbers, but Merv had a

Alex was not only bright, but he was also cute. I can't help but wonder who was responsible for the suits we used to wear!

contract, so the show stayed on. They used to tape across the hall from us, and I'd walk over to check it out. They would have no audience. They wanted one, but it was just that the show was so dull, nobody wanted to come in to see it. Some guy would spin the wheel and it would spin forever, then he'd say, "Give me an L." There'd be no L and the next contestant would spin the wheel forever and on it went.

Chuck Woolery was the host of the show, and Dean Craig, who was an executive at NBC, asked me to see if I could figure out what he was doing wrong and give him some pointers. I knew Chuck from the days when he was married to Jo Ann Pflug and used to sit in the audience while she did *The Hollywood Squares*. Well, I watched him work, and it was true—he seemed to be doing everything wrong—but for some reason it worked. In fact, he was adorable. "Leave him alone," I told Dean. "He'll be fine."

I know I was right, because recently I was talking to Chuck and he told me that when I was renegotiating my contract with Heatter/Quigley, Merrill approached him about possibly taking my place as host of *The Hollywood Squares*. Chuck was flattered but explained that he was already hosting *Wheel of Fortune*. According to Chuck, Merrill said, "Forget *Wheel of Fortune*. It will never last."

Anyway, Lin Bolen eventually left NBC, and in came our old nemesis, Fred Silverman. We'd been in the 11:30 slot from the beginning and I think he was pissed off that we were still on the air, so what did he do? Well, he couldn't very well cancel us—we were still doing pretty well for NBC—so he decided to fix that. In October 1976, he changed our time slot. We were moved back one hour to 10:30, which put us up against *The Price Is Right*. That was a tough slot, but after a couple of years, our audience found us again, so in October 1978, Mr. Silverman moved us to 1:00. Just in case we were getting too comfy in that time slot, he moved us again in March 1979, this time to 12:30. I guess our numbers still weren't bad enough for him, because in August of that same year, he put us back to 10:30, fighting once again with *The Price Is Right*.

Finally, in June 1980, Fred decided to take care of us, once and for all. He cleared an hour and a half in the middle of the day for a new show, *The David Letterman Show*. This was really innovative daytime television. Unfortunately, innovative isn't always good. I told Jay Michaels, who was a vice president over there, to get ready for some single-digit shares. He just laughed, but not for long. I'm not saying David Letterman isn't brilliant, which he is—as the success of his late-night show proves—but his audience was absolutely not the same audience that watched game shows during the day. When they canceled *The Hollywood Squares,* we still had a 20 rating and a 27 share. In no time at all, the same time slot was getting a 9 rating. So they quickly canceled a half-hour of it, leaving the studio with another problem. What would they put on for that half-hour?

Well, *Wheel of Fortune* was one of the shows canceled to make room for *Letterman.* They were in the midst of their wrap party when the execs ran down to the set and announced they were renewing the show. This opened things up for Merv to negotiate a whole new contract, which, knowing Merv, I'm sure was a great one. In fact, his deal was so good, the network claimed they had no money left for the raise that host Chuck Woolery asked for. He refused to go back unless his salary went up, so they decided to hire the kid who did the weather, Pat Sajak. It didn't seem to matter what they did to *Wheel of Fortune,* it just went on and on. Not so for the daytime *Letterman Show,* though. By October, it was gone, but, of course, so were we, at least as far as the network was concerned.

When Silverman canceled us, everybody was very sad, except me. I remember thinking, this is not the end of something—it's the beginning of something new. That's always been my philosophy and I've never panicked. And why should I have? This was not like being a young actor whose play has finished its run. I'd been working for fifteen years straight and I still had a year to go in syndication—for which I would be paid very well—so it wasn't a money issue. I guess I was just sad to see a good thing end.

The celebrity panel on that last NBC show consisted of Rose Marie, Tom Poston, Michele Lee, Vincent Price, Leslie Uggams, George Gobel, Marty Allen, Charlie Callas, and Wayland Flowers & Madame in the center square. When the last show was almost done, I asked everybody to say something and when I got to Wayland & Madame he said something appropriate, and then Madame piped up with, "This is our last week and I'm very sad about that, because I tried to save the show. I even slept with Fred Silverman. And I told him, I said, Fred, you can screw some of the people some of the time, but you can't screw all of the people all of the time." Of course, we didn't put that on the air, but somebody has it on tape. I sure wish that someone were me.

17

The Year in Vegas

Stories from our last year on the air.

When *The Hollywood Squares* finally got canceled by NBC, it was still very popular and an easy sale in syndication, so we made a deal with Meshulam Riklis (everyone called him Rick), who owned the Riviera Hotel in Las Vegas. He not only paid for the complete production, but also provided accommodations for our regular stars and the production people. We shot the show in the main showroom during the day and were able to get a lot of good bookings by using stars who were already appearing in Vegas.

The thing I really enjoyed about that year was having guys on the show such as Shecky Green and Henny Youngman, who just killed me, they were so funny. Of course, the same old problem crept up. They just couldn't understand that we needed to get a certain number of questions in each show in order to make it work. I'd tell Henny to make a quick joke, then answer the question. He'd nod that he understood. Then I'd ask Henny a question and he'd start doing a monologue. I'd look around for Jay Redack, our producer, and he was nowhere to be seen. Then I'd try to locate Quig— also among the missing.

Turned out, they were at the $500 blackjack table and had no intention of coming in to the taping. It was a far cry from the old days when Merrill and Bob were involved in every aspect of the show and the line producers were always on their toes. By the time we went to Vegas, the show was tired. Merrill and Bob had a lot of other irons in the fire and figured *Squares,* their oldest living child, had been around long enough to get by on its own. This is what made that last year so difficult. I was pretty much left to my own devices to make the show run smoothly.

It was also tough on our director, Jerry Shaw, and his crew. They were used to having a dedicated set at NBC. For fifteen years, they'd come in and everything would be there. Not so at the Riviera. Every morning at six o'clock, the show had to be set up. That meant completely constructing the set, the electronics, the lights, and everything else it took to make the show work. Then, every afternoon, we had to strike the set to make room for the show that would be coming in that night.

Most of our production people had families who they had to spend a lot of time away from during that Las Vegas year, and it could get pretty lonely, so some of them would amuse themselves at the gaming tables. One night, Harry Friedman had been playing blackjack and was doing pretty well. He got on an elevator with a bunch of hundred-dollar chips in his hand. A woman got on right after him who looked like a schoolteacher from Oregon. She smiled at him, he smiled back, and then she said, "Are you as lonely as you look?"

Harry was a little taken aback by this. "How lonely do I look?" Finally he started to catch on. He held up a hundred-dollar chip. "Do I look this lonely?"

"No," she answered. "You look twice that lonely."

Paul Lynde, with his prima donna attitude, didn't help make that year any easier, either. Christmas week is always a busy time in Vegas and the Riviera was renovating the hotel, so everybody had to give up their suites and take regular rooms. These were nice enough rooms and it really didn't seem to bother anyone—except Paul. He got on the phone and demanded a suite. I told him to forget it, that there weren't any suites available. He looked at me, hung up the phone, and said, "Did you know my house is in *Architectural Digest*?" I told him I really hadn't been aware of that fact. "Well, it is," he said, grandly gesturing around his room. "And you expect me to live like this?"

During the year we shot in Vegas, we all caught as many shows as we could. Of course, none of us missed the opportunity to see Glen Campbell when he headlined at the Riviera. In the audience were his parents, who he proceeded to bring on stage. They performed two numbers, "Silver Haired Daddy of Mine" and "Crying Time." Well, the old folks were wonderful and they brought the house down. A little later in the show, Glen called Paul out of the audience and introduced him.

"You're so funny," he said. "You should have your own act in Vegas."

"Can't do it," said Paul.

"Why not?" Glen asked.

"Because," said Paul, in his own inimitable way, "both of *my* parents are dead."

Phyllis McGuire, who was one of the McGuire Sisters and a very old friend of mine, threw us a lovely dinner party at her Las Vegas home, which happens to be a veritable fortress. So a bunch of us from the show were all sitting at this giant dining room table, surrounded by priceless art and antiques, and Paul turned to Phyllis and said, "You have such expensive things. Don't you ever worry about break-ins?" Well, Phyllis reached under the table and pressed a button, and suddenly a steel wall came down around the entire house and hit the ground with a bang. Everyone at the table jumped. After a few moments of silence, Paul piped up, "Gee, I sure hope the pussycat wasn't leavin'."

Phyllis appeared as a guest star during that time and I was so happy to see her there. Everybody was getting pretty casual about the show, stars weren't really dressing up, and sometimes our contestants, chosen from the audience, were in those ridiculous tourist outfits people seem to wear only when visiting Las Vegas. When Phyllis showed up, she looked like a million bucks and probably was wearing it in jewelry alone. Then I started reading her questions. Well, I've never seen questions so hard. I swear, some of them would have stumped Gore Vidal—but Phyllis came through like the champ she was. How she knew the answers to those questions, I'll never know, but she did.

One day, we had Joan Rivers, Suzanne Somers, all four Lennon Sisters, and Pia Zadora, who was married to Riklis, on the show. Out they came to be introduced to the audience, and all seven women had their hair done up in a side ponytail, a style that was very popular at the time. Joan was horrified and immediately went back to hair and makeup for a new do, but there wasn't time to redo everyone before the first taping, so the others just had to go with it.

The cast members spent a lot of time in the casinos. At times George Gobel would be playing blackjack at four in the morning, hitting on twenty, and we'd know he'd had enough. That's when Harry or Jay or I would carry him to his room and pour him into bed. But no matter how much he drank or stayed up late, he never missed a call, was never late to a taping, and never blew a joke. And he sure made that last year in Vegas a lot more fun for me.

The gambling did a lot of people in, including yours truly. Gobel and I used to like to sit around the hotel bar drinking with the hookers. Sometimes one of them would have to leave for an hour or so; then she'd come back and there we'd be, still drinking. One night, we got a little too bombed and Gobel went to bed. I decided I was still too wound up to go to sleep, so I stopped at the roulette table. Now, that's a game it's pretty hard to win a lot of money at, but I guess the saints look after children and drunks, because I won $18,000 that night. What I did next can be described as one of my more stupid moves. Instead of taking it to the cage and having it locked up, I took it to my room. The next morning, it was gone. I'm still convinced it was an inside job, but I'm grateful I had passed out. If I had awakened during the robbery, somebody might have shot me. That morning, I took a long, hard look at myself. I wasn't looking as good as I used to; my wife, Sally, and I weren't getting along; and I had just lost $18,000. That's when I decided it was time to stop drinking, and I haven't had a drink since. So I guess you could say a bad thing turned into a good thing for me.

In a way, I'm almost sorry we took *The Hollywood Squares* to Vegas. Maybe it would have been better to let it go out with a bang on NBC. On the other hand, I think if I could do one more year of that great show with all those wonderful people, I'd be happy to do it on the moon.

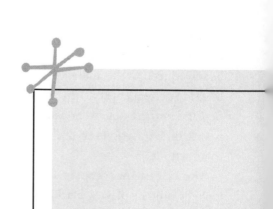

18

My Favorite Jokes

The one-liners that kept me laughing.

Many lists have been floating around the Internet about Peter Marshall's favorite jokes from *The Hollywood Squares*. Well, I've seen a lot of these jokes and they're very good, but I've never made a list of my favorite jokes for anybody—until now.

So here they are, for whatever the reason, the jokes from *The Hollywood Squares* that I loved the most.

Q: Rubbing an alligator's stomach has a curious effect on him. What does rubbing his tummy make him do?

Paul Lynde: Eat you.

Q: Is it a good sign if your man loves animals?

Joan Rivers: Not to excess.

Q: You're in the woods with a friend and a snake bites him. What's the first thing you should do?

Paul: Find a new friend.

Q: In 1931, two men in Russia slapped each other in the face continually for three hundred hours. Why?

Marty Allen: Just a lover's quarrel.

Q: Anthony Quinn thinks they should be abolished, but he wouldn't turn one down. What are they?

Paul: Fifty-year-old women.

Q: The raccoon does something before he eats that few other animals do. What?

Jim Brolin: He has a cocktail.

Q: Can guinea pigs whistle?

Paul: Only when they come to a boil.

Q: The French call it "wooden mouth." What do you call it?

Paul: I don't know but it'll cost you extra.

Q: In English, we know the three daughters of Zeus as Joy, Bloom, and Brilliance. Together they're known as the three . . . what?

Vincent Price: The three little pigs.

Q: According to Greek mythology, the god Apollo, in love with the maiden Daphne, pursued her through the forest. When he caught up with her, what did she change into?

Mel Brooks: Something comfortable.

Q: The palms of your hands are turning yellow. What have you probably been doing too much?

Paul: Massaging my gardener.

Q: When this happens to you, you should think of it as nature's way of telling you to slow down. What is it?

Paul: The last rites.

Q: What would you call a chicken that's cut up, stewed, and served in its own gravy?

Paul: Mortally wounded.

Q: Can intense pleasure bring on a heart attack?

Rose Marie: How would I know?

Q: What fictional character ran around screaming, "I'm late, I'm late"?

Paul: That was Alice, and her mother's sick about it.

Q: True or false? It's illegal to spank children in Sweden.

Paul: Hell, just take them to Germany.

Q: What was your grandmother trying to do when she drank a mixture of kerosene, sugar, and onion juice?

George: We never knew. She blew up.

Q: Julie Andrews said that at the age of twelve, she discovered something of hers was as developed as that of a grown woman. What was it?

Paul: Unfortunately, it was her brother.

Q: True or false? Runny noses are good for you.

George: Good for me—bad for a professional harmonica player.

Q: In yoga, when a person crosses his legs, entwines them under him, and tucks his heels up into his groin, what's it called?

Charley Weaver: It's still called a groin, but it looks different.

Q: What is a female bullfighter in Mexico called?

Charley: Before the last fight she was called José Garcia.

Q: There's a man and a woman standing in front of you, of about the same size and weight. Whose body contains more water?

George: The one that's hopping.

Q: Is there any reason why a doctor would use a tuning fork while giving you an examination?

Paul: No, the tuning fork was my idea.

Q: True or false? A Canadian doctor successfully transplanted a man's big toe onto his thumb.

Paul: That's how dull it can get in Canada.

Q: Is it ever necessary for a woman to divulge her private, innermost secrets to her doctor?

Paul: It doesn't matter. He's gonna see 'em anyway.

Q: When a couple has a baby, who is responsible for its sex?
Charley: I'll lend him the car. The rest is up to him.

Q: When a child begins to get curious about sex, what is the one question he will most ask his mommy and daddy?
Paul: Where can I get some?

And here's the joke that makes me laugh every time I think about it. I don't know why, but it's my favorite joke of all.

Q: What is the definition of the word "gobbledygook"?
George: That's the stuff you'll find in the corner of a turkey's eye.

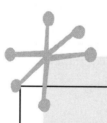

19

Everybody Who Ever Did the Show (I Hope)

A very long list of celebrities who appeared on *The Hollywood Squares* over the years.

The *Hollywood Squares* was a unique show in many ways. I believe that it was the first written comedy game show. I'm also pretty sure, between daytime, nighttime, syndicated, and *Storybook Squares*, that we probably used more stars than any other show on television.

My goal is to try to list all of those stars so that fans of the show can peruse it at their leisure. Maybe seeing a certain name will spark a memory of an individual show, or even an individual question or joke. The big problem was the Las Vegas year. There were no listings of stars in *TV Guide*, and I couldn't dig up any cast sheets, so I'm probably missing a few names. For this, I apologize in advance.

I almost didn't attempt this chapter, because I was so worried about leaving somebody out. But it's something that hasn't been done before and I just couldn't resist the temptation, so this is what I'd like to propose. If anyone out there was on the show and I left your name out, please contact me. You can reach me at my website at www.boysinger.com. I will issue a public apology *and* take you to lunch.

Aames, Willie	Albert, Edward	Allen, Elizabeth
Aaron, Hank	Albertson, Jack	Allen, Marty
Adams, Don	Albright, Lola	Allen, Steve
Adams, Edie	Alexander, Denise	Allyson, June
Adams, Jeb	Allan, Jed	Ames, Ed
Adams, Nick	Allen, Byron	Amsterdam, Morey
Adotta, Kip	Allen, Debbie	Amory, Cleveland

Amos, John
Anderson, Barbara
Anderson, Daryl
Anderson, Loni
Anderson, Lynn
Anderson, Melissa
    Sue
Anderson, Richard
Andrews, Tige
Andrews, Tina
Anka, Paul
Anton, Susan
Archerd, Army
Arden, Eve
Arkin, Adam
Arnaz, Desi Jr.
Arnaz, Lucie
Arnold, Danny
Arquette, Cliff (as
    Charley Weaver)
Arquette, Rosanna
Arrants, Rod
Arthur, Maureen
Ashley, Elizabeth
Asner, Ed
Avalon, Frankie
Backus, Jim
Baddeley, Hermione
Baer, Max
Baggetta, Vincent
Bailey, Pearl
Bailey, Peter
Bailey, Raymond
Bain, Barbara
Bain, Conrad

Baio, Scott
Baker, Diane
Ballard, Kaye
Barbeau, Adrienne
Barkley, Roger
Barnes, Priscilla
Barnstable, Cyb
Barnstable, Tricia
Baron, Sandy
Barrett, Rona
Barry, Gene
Bates, Rhonda
Bauer, Jaime Lyn
Baxter, Anne
Baxter-Birney,
    Meredith
Bayer Sager, Carole
Beatty, Ned
Benedict, Dirk
Benet, Brenda
Bennett, Joan
Benton, Barbi
Bergen, Polly
Berger, Senta
Berle, Milton
Berman, Shelley
Bernardi, Herschel
Berry, Fred
Berry, Ken
Bertinelli, Valerie
Big Bird
Birney, David
Bishop, Elvin
Bishop, Joey
Bixby, Bill

Blair, Janet
Blake, Amanda
Blake, Robert
Blanchard, Susan
Bluestone, Ed
Bono, Sonny
Boone, Pat
Boosler, Elayne
Borge, Victor
Borgnine, Ernest
Bosley, Tom
Boxleitner, Bruce
Braden, Vic
Braver, Billy
Braverman, Bart
Brazzi, Rossano
Bregman, Tracey
Brennan, Eileen
Brenner, David
Bridges, Beau
Bridges, Lloyd
Bridges, Todd
Brill, Marty
Brogan, Jimmy
Brolin, James
Brooks, Albert
Brooks, Foster
Brooks, Mel
Brothers, Dr. Joyce
Brown, Jim
Brown, Johnny
Brown, Robert
Buckley, Betty
Bull, Richard
Buono, Victor

Burghoff, Gary
Burr, Raymond
Burton, LeVar
Buttons, Red
Buttram, Pat
Buzzi, Ruth
Byner, John
Cabot, Sebastian
Caesar, Sid
Callan, Mickey
Callas, Charlie
Cambridge, Godfrey
Campbell, Glen
Campanella, Joseph
Cannon, Dyan
Cannon, Freddy
Canova, Diana
Canova, Judy
Captain Kangaroo
Carey, Macdonald
Carey, Ron
Carlin, George
Carmel, Roger
Carne, Judy
Carr, Darleen
Carr, Vikki
Carroll, Diahann
Carroll, James
Carter, Billy
Carter, Jack
Carter, Lynda
Cartwright, Angela
Cash, June Carter
Cassidy, Jack
Cassidy, Joanna

Cassidy, Ted
Castellano, Richard
Cauthen, Steve
Chad & Jeremy
Chaffee, Suzy
Chamberlain, Wilt
Channing, Carol
Chapman, Graham
Charisse, Cyd
Charo
Charles, Ray
Cheech & Chong
Cher
Chic
Christopher, William
Clark, Candy
Clark, Dick
Clark, Fred
Clark, Petula
Clark, Roy
Clark, Susan
Clary, Robert
Claus, Santa
Clayton, Bob
Clinger, Debra
Coca, Imogene
Coco, James
Colbert, Bob
Cole, Dennis
Cole, Michael
Cole, Tina
Collins, Pat
Commodores
Conn, Didi
Connelly, Chris

Connors, Mike
Conrad, Robert
Conrad, William
Constantine, Michael
Conway, Tim
Cooney, Dennis
Cooper, Alice
Corby, Ellen
Cord, Alex
Coelho, Susie
Cox, Ronny
Cox, Wally
Crane, Bob
Crenna, Richard
Cristal, Linda
Crosby, Cathy Lee
Crosby, Mary
Crosby, Norm
Crystal, Billy
Cullen, Bill
Culp, Robert
Cummings, Bob
Cummings, Quinn
Curtis, Jamie Lee
Dailey, Irene
Daily, Bill
Dalton, Abby
Dalton, Leslie
Damon, Cathryn
Damone, Vic
Dana, Vic
Dangerfield, Rodney
Danza, Tony
Dark, Johnny
Darren, James

Davidson, John
Davis, Ann B.
Davis, Billy
Davis, Jim
Davis, Mac
Davis, Phyllis
Davis, Sammy Jr.
Day, Laraine
Dean, Jimmy
Dee, Kiki
Dee, Sandra
DeLuise, Dom
Denver, Bob
Deuel, Peter
Deutsch, Patti
DeWitt, Joyce
Dey, Susan
Diller, Phyllis
Dimitri, Richard
Dino, Desi, & Billy
Dishy, Bob
Dickinson, Angie
Dickson, Brenda
Dobson, Kevin
Dors, Diana
Douglas, Mike
Downs, Hugh
Doyle, David
Dreesen, Tom
Dru, Joanne
Drury, James
DuBois, Ja'net
Duff, Howard
Duffy, Patrick
Dufour, Val

Dugan, Dennis
Duke, Patty
Dullea, Keir
Duncan, Sandy
Dunn, Michael
Durante, Jimmy
   (cameo)
Dussault, Nancy
Eden, Barbara
Eder, Shirley
Edwards, Ralph
   (cameo)
Edwards, Stephanie
Edwards, Vince
Ekland, Britt
Elder, Ann
Elliman, Yvonne
Elliot, Cass
Ely, Ron
Enberg, Dick
England Dan & John
   Ford Coley
Erving, Julius (Dr. J)
Esposito, Phil
Estrada, Erik
Eubanks, Bob
Evans, Mike
Everett, Chad
Fabares, Shelley
Fabray, Nannette
Fabian
Fairbanks, Douglas Jr.
Falana, Lola
Falk, Peter
Farentino, James

Fargas, Antonio
Fargo, Donna
Farr, Felicia
Farr, Jamie
Farrell, Mike
Farrell, Sharon
Feldman, Marty
Feldon, Barbara
Fell, Norman
Fender, Freddy
Ferrigno, Lou
Field, Sally
Fields, Totie
Fisher, Gail
Flack, Roberta
Flagg, Fannie
Flanagan, Fionnula
Flannery, Susan
Fleming, Art
Fletcher, Louise
Flintstone, Fred
Flowers, Wayland
   (Madame, Jiffy,
   Macklehoney,
   Smedley)
Flynn, Joe
Fontaine, Frank
Fontane, Char
Ford, Glenn
Ford, Phil
Ford, Tennessee Ernie
Foreman, George
Forrest, Steve
Forsyth, Rosemary
Forsythe, John

Foxworth, Robert
Foxx, Redd
Francis, Connie
Franciosa, Tony
Franciscus, James
Franklin, Aretha
Franklin, Bonnie
Fridell, Squire
Fuller, Robert
Funicello, Annette
Furst, Stephen
Gabor, Eva
Gabor, Zsa Zsa
Gail, Max
Garr, Teri
Garver, Kathy
Gary, John
Gatlin, Larry
Gautier, Dick
Gaye, Marvin
Gayle, Jackie
Gazzara, Ben
Geer, Will
George, Christopher
George, Lynda Day
George, Phyllis
George, Susan
Gerard, Gil
Gerritsen, Lisa
Ghostley, Alice
Gibson, Althea
Gibson, Henry
Gilbert, Melissa
Gilford, Gwynne
Gilliam, Stu

Gingold, Hermione
Glass, Kathy
Glass, Ron
Gobel, George
Godfrey, Arthur
Goldsboro, Bobby
Goldsmith, Sydney
Golonka, Arlene
Goodeve, Grant
Gorney, Karen
Gordon, Gale
Gorshin, Frank
Goulet, Robert
Grable, Betty
Graham, Virginia
Granger, Farley
Grant, Lee
Grassle, Karen
Graves, Peter
Graves, Teresa
Gray, Erin
Gray, Linda
Greene, Lorne
Greene, Shecky
Gregory, James
Grey, Joel
Grier, Pam
Griffin, Merv
Groh, David
Guardino, Harry
Guillaume, Robert
Guthrie, Janet
Guthrie, Richard
Gwynne, Fred
Gypsy Rose Lee

Haber, Joyce
Hackett, Buddy
Hackman, Gene
Haggerty, Dan
Hagman, Larry
Hall, Andrea
Hall, Deidre
Hall, Monty
Hamill, Dorothy
Hamilton, George
Hamlisch, Marvin
Handleman, Stanley
Myron
Harper, Ron
Harper, Valerie
Harrington, Pat
Harris, Julie
Harrison, Noel
Hartley, Mariette
Hartman, David
Harty, Patricia
Haskell, Peter
Hayes, Bill
Hayes, Helen
Haynes, Lloyd
Hays, Kathryn
Hays, Robert
Heatherton, Joey
Hedison, David
Hegyes, Robert
Hemphill, Shirley
Hemsley, Sherman
Henderson, Florence
Henning, Linda Kaye
Henry, Pat

Hensley, Pamela
Hickman, Dwayne
Hines, Connie
Hines, Mimi
Holliman, Earl
Hope, Bob (cameo)
Hornung, Paul
Howard, Ken
Howard, Ron
Howard, Susan
Howe, Gordie
Howes, Sally Ann
Howland, Beth
Hudson Brothers
Hudson, Rock
Hunter, Tab
Hutchins, Will
Ireland, Jill
Isacksen, Peter
Jackson, Kate
Jackson, Reggie
James, Art
James, Dennis
Jensen, Karen
Jensen, Maren
Jessel, George
Johnson, Arte
Johnson, Jay
Johnson, Marques
Johnson, Van
Jones, Burt
Jones, Carolyn
Jones, Christine
Jones, Dean
Jones, George

Jones, Jack
Jones, Shirley
Jordan, James Carroll
Joseph, Jackie
Jump, Gordon
Kanaly, Steve
Kaplan, Gabe
Kastner, Peter
Kaufman, Andy
Kavner, Julie
Kay, Dianne
Kaye, Caren
Kazan, Lainie
KC (without the
    Sunshine Band)
Kelton, Bobby
Keeshan, Bob
Keith, Susan
Kelly, Brian
Kelly, Jack
Kelly, Roz
Kelsey, Linda
Kelton, Bob
Kennedy, George
Kennedy, Jayne
Kennedy, Tom
Kercheval, Ken
Kershaw, Doug
Kerwin, Lance
Khan, Chaka
Kiel, Richard
King, Alan
King, Evelyn
    "Champagne"
Kirby, George

Kitt, Eartha
Klein, Robert
Klemperer, Werner
Klous, Pat
Klugman, Jack
Knight, Gladys
Knight, Ted
Knotts, Don
Kopell, Bernie
Korman, Harvey
Kulp, Nancy
Lahr, Bert
Laine, Frankie
Lamas, Fernando
Lamour, Dorothy
Landau, Martin
Lander, David L.
Landers, Audrey
Landers, Judy
Landesberg, Steve
Landon, Michael
Langdon, Sue Anne
Lane, Sara
Lange, Hope
Lange, Ted
Lane, Abbe
La Rosa, Julius
Lavin, Linda
Lawford, Peter
Lawrence, Carol
Lawrence, Vicki
Leachman, Cloris
Learned, Michael
Leary, Brianne
Lee, Brenda

Lee, Michele
Leigh, Janet
Lemmon, Chris
Lemon, Meadowlark
Lennon, Diane
Lennon, Janet
Lennon, Kathy
Lennon, Peggy
Leno, Jay
Leonard, Jack E.
Leonard, Sugar Ray
Letterman, David
Lewis, Jerry (cameo)
Lewis, Marcia
Lewis, Richard
Lewis, Shari
Ligon, Tom
Linden, Hal
Lindsey, George
Linkletter, Art
Linville, Larry
Lipton, Peggy
Little Anthony
Little Feat
Little, Rich
Lockhart, Anne
Lockhart, June
Lohman, Al
London, Julie
Long, Richard
Lopes, Davey
Lopez, Priscilla
Loren, Donna
Love, Mike
Lovell, Andrea Hall

Lund, Deanna
Luft, Lorna
Luz, Franc
Lynde, Janice
Lynde, Paul
Lynn, Loretta
Lynley, Carol
Lyon, Sue
MacArthur, James
MacGregor,
    Katherine
Mackenzie, Beverly
MacKenzie, Gisele
MacLeod, Gavin
MacLeod, Patti
MacNee, Patrick
MacRae, Meredith
MacRae, Sheila
Macy, Bill
Maharis, George
Majors, Lee
Mallory, Victoria
Malone, Moses
Manchester, Melissa
Mandan, Robert
Mandrell, Barbara
Manners. Mickey
Mantle, Mickey
Marlowe, Hugh
Marshall, E. G.
Marshall Tucker Band
Martin, Billy
Martin, Gail
Martin, Pamela Sue
Martin, Ross

Martin, Steve
Martin, Tony
Martindale, Wink
Martino, Al
Marx, Groucho
Mason, Marsha
Mason, Pamela
Mason, Jackie
Masters, Marie
Matheson, Tim
Mathis, Johnny
Mathis, Sherry
Matthau, Walter
Mayo, Whitman
McCallum, David
McCarthy, Kevin
McClanahan, Rue
McConnell, Judith
McCoo, Marilyn
McCook, John
McCord, Kent
McDowall, Roddy
McGovern, Maureen
McGuire, Phyllis
McKean, Michael
McKeon, Phillip
McKrell, Jim
McKuen, Rod
McMahon, Ed
McNair, Barbara
McNichol, Kristy
McWhirter, Julie
Meadows, Audrey
Meadows, Jayne
Meara, Anne

Mears, Rick
Medford, Kay
Melville, Sam
Menzies, Heather
Meriwether, Lee
Merman, Ethel
Merritt, Theresa
Messing, Shep
Michaels, Marilyn
Michaelson, Melissa
Miles, Vera
Milland, Ray
Miller, Ann
Miller, Cheryl
Miller, George
Miller, Roger
Mills, Juliet
Milner, Martin
Mitchell, Scoey
The Monkees (without Peter Tork)
Monkhouse, Bob
Montalban, Ricardo
Monteith, Kelly
Montgomery, Belinda J.
Montgomery, Elizabeth
Moore, Dudley (cameo)
Moore, Garry
Moore, Roger
Moorehead, Agnes
Moran, Erin
Moreno, Rita

Morgan, Jaye P.
Morita, Pat
Morris, Garrett
Morris, Greg
Morris, Howard
Morse, Robert
Most, Donny
Muldowney, Shirley
Mule Deer, Gary
Mulhare, Edward
Mull, Martin
Mulligan, Richard
Murdock, George
Murray, Jan
Nabors, Jim
Narz, Jack
Naud, Melinda
Navratilova, Martina
Nelson, Harriet
Nelson, Ozzie
New Birth
Newhart, Bob
Newley, Anthony
Newman, Barry
Newton, Connie
Nicholas, Denise
Nightingale, Maxine
Nimoy, Leonard
Norris, Christopher
North, Jay
Nuyen, France
Nye, Louis
Oakes, Randi
O'Brian, Hugh
O'Brien, David

O'Connor, Donald
O'Connor, Glynnis
O'Grady, Lani
O'Hara, Maureen
Olsen, Merlin
O'Neill, Jennifer
Oscar the Grouch
O'Shea, Tessie
Osmond, Donny
Osmond, Marie
Owens, Buck
Page, Patti
Paige, Janis
Palance, Jack
Palillo, Ron
Paluzzi, Luciana
Parton, Dolly
Patterson, Dick
Patterson, Floyd
Patterson, Melody
Peaches & Herb
Pearl, Minnie
Perry, John Bennett
Pescow, Donna
Peters, Audrey
Peters, Bernadette
Pettet, Joanna
Peyser, Penny
Pflug, Jo Ann
Phillips, Mackenzie
Phillips, Wendy
Piekarski, Julie
Pincay, Lafit Jr.
Pinkerton, Nancy
Place, Mary Kay

Plato, Dana
Platt, Ed
Pleshette, Suzanne
Plumb, Eve
Podell, Rick
Pointer, Bonnie
Poston, Tom
Potts, Annie
Potts, Cliff
Powell, Jane
Powers, Stefanie
Prather, Joan
Price, Vincent
Principal, Victoria
Prinze, Freddie
Prowse, Juliet
Purcell, Sarah
Rae, Charlotte
Randall, Tony
Rankin, Kenny
Rawls, Lou
Rayburn, Gene
Raye, Martha
Raymond, Gene
Redeker, Quinn
Redgrave, Lynn
Reed, Robert
Reese, Della
Reeves, Martha
Regina, Paul
Reid, Tim
Reilly, Charles Nelson
Reiner, Carl
Reiner, Rob
Reuben, Dr. David

Rey, Alejandro
Reynolds, Burt
Reynolds, Debbie
Rhoades, Barbara
Rhue, Madlyn
Rich, Adam
Richardson, Susan
Rickles, Don
Rigby, Cathy
Rigg, Diana
Riggs, Bobby
Riley, Jeannie C.
Riley, Jeanine
Ritter, John
Rivers, Joan
Roberts, Doris
Roberts, Tony
Robertson, Cliff
Robertson, Dale
Rodgers, Pamela
Roger & Roger
Rogers, Ginger
Rogers, Kenny
Rogers, Roy
Rogers, Wayne
Rolle, Esther
The Rollers
Romero, Cesar
Rooney, Mickey
Rose Marie
Ross, Marion
Rossi, Steve
Roundtree, Richard
Rubble, Barney
Rudolph, Wilma

Rundgren, Todd
Rush, Barbara
Russell, Bill
Russell, Jane
Russell, Kurt
Ryan, Irene
Rydell, Bobby
Sahl, Mort
Sainte-Marie, Buffy
Sales, Soupy
Salt, Jennifer
Saluga, Bill
Sanders, George
Sanders, Richard
Sanford, Isabel
Sang, Samantha
Santos, Joe
Sargent, Dick
Savalas, Telly
Saxon, John
Schreiber, Avery
Schuck, John
Scott, Debralee
Scott, George C.
Seaforth-Hayes, Susan
Seagren, Bob
Seals & Crofts
Sellecca, Connie
Severinsen, Doc
Sharma, Barbara
Shatner, William
Shawn, Dick
Sheldon, Jack
Sherman, Allan
Sherman, Bobby

Shore, Dinah
Shortridge, Stephen
Simmons, Jean
Simpson, O.J.
Sinatra, Frank Jr.
Sinatra, Nancy
Sinatra, Tina
Silvers, Phil
Skiles & Henderson
Smith, Kate
Smith, Margo
Smith, Martha
Smith, Robyn
Smith, Roger
Smith, Shelley
Smith, William
Smothers, Dick
Sokol, Marilyn
Somers, Suzanne
Sommer, Elke
Sommers, Joanie
Soo, Jack
Spang, Laurette
Spitz, Mark
Stabler, Ken
Stafford, Jim
Stafford, Susan
Stapleton, Jean
Stapleton, Maureen
Starbuck, Jo Jo
Stargard
Steinberg, David
Stephenson, Skip
Stevens, Andrew
Stevens, Connie

Stevens, Kaye
Stevens, Paul
Stevens, Shawn
Stevens, Stella
Stevenson, McLean
Stewart, John
Stiller, Jerry
St. Jacques, Raymond
St. James, Susan
St. John, Jill
Storch, Larry
Strasberg, Susan
Struthers, Sally
Stuart, Mary
Sues, Alan
Sullivan, Susan
Susann, Jacqueline
Swan, Tommy
Swann, Lynn
Swanson, Miss Gloria
Swit, Loretta
Tacker, Francine
Tarkenton, Fran
Tayback, Vic
Taylor, Josh
Taylor, Rip
Taylor, Rod
Terry-Thomas
Tewes, Lauren
Thomas, Danny
Tighe, Kevin
Tillis, Mel
Tilton, Charlene
Tiny Tim
Tomlin, Lily

Tomme, Ron
Torres, Liz
Travalena, Fred
Travolta, Ellen
Travolta, Joey
Treacher, Arthur
Trebek, Alex
Truman, Margaret
Tubes
Tucker, Tanya
Turner, Tina
UFO
Uggams, Leslie
Urich, Robert
Vaccaro, Brenda
Vale, Jerry
Valli, Frankie
Van Ark, Joan
Van Buren, Abigail
Vance, Vivian
Van Devere, Trish
Van Doren, Mamie
Van Dyke, Dick
Van Patten, Dick
Van Patten, Jim
Van Patten, Nels
Van Patten, Pat
Van Patten, Vince
Vaughn, Robert
Vee, Bobby
Verdugo, Elena
Vernon, Jackie
Vigoda, Abe
Villechaize, Herve
Vinton, Bobby

Waggoner, Lyle
Walden, Robert
Walker, Jimmie
Walker, Nancy
Wallace, Marcia
Walley, Deborah
Wallis, Shani
Walsh, Lory
Walter, Jessica
Walters, Laurie
Walton, Bill
War
Ward, Burt
Warren, Lesley Ann
Warwick, Dionne
Wayne, Carol
Wayne, Pat
Weaver, Dennis

Webb, Jack
West, Adam
West, Dottie
White, Betty
Wilde, Cornel
Willard, Fred
Williams, Anson
Williams, Paul
Williams, Van
Williamson, Fred
Wilson, Demond
Wilson, Earl
Wilson, Flip
Wilson, Nancy
Winchell, Paul (and
   Jerry Mahoney)
Winters, Jonathan
Winters, Shelley

Withers, Jane
Wolfman Jack
Wood, Kelly
Woods, Ren
Woolery, Chuck
Wopat, Tom
Worley, JoAnne
Wyman, Jane
Wynette, Tammy
Wynter, Dana
Yates, Stephen
York, Susannah
Young, Donna Jean
Young, Gig
Youngman, Henny
Yune, Johnny
Zadora, Pia

Every single one of these people contributed in their own special way to making *The Hollywood Squares* the great show it was. With the exception of the births of my children and grandchildren, and meeting and marrying Laurie, I'd say hosting it was definitely the highlight of my life.

At the end of our run, my psychic powers told me it wasn't over for *The Hollywood Squares* and me. I really believed I would someday be doing the show again. When it was announced that there would be an hour block called *Match Game/ Hollywood Squares Hour*, I was sure they'd offer it to me, especially since Gene Rayburn was hosting *Match Game*. Of course, that didn't happen, and Jon Bauman hosted the show. I kind of hate to admit that I was happy when it didn't even last one season.

Then, in 1986 the show was revived again. I waited for the call, but it went to John Davidson instead. Even though I was disappointed, I was thrilled for John and thought he did a very good job. That show lasted until 1989. Of course, by 1998, when the show resurfaced once more, I realized I wasn't going to be the host of *The Hollywood Squares* ever again, but somehow, I never really said goodbye to the show.

At the end of each taping, after Kenny Williams finished his rapid-fire announcement of prizes and bye-bye gifts, we all waited for the producer to say the three little words that let us know the show was over: "It's a wrap!"

Each time I heard those words, they signified the end of a small chapter of my life. It was fun to hear them because it meant I could pack up my gear and go home or go out and have a drink with my friends. It was also kind of sad, because every time those words were said, we moved one show closer to the inevitable end of our run.

Putting this book together gave me the opportunity to sit down with some old friends from *Squares*, some of whom I hadn't seen in years, and rehash those happy times. We talked about things that happened during the long run of the show, about all the fun we used to have, about the wonderful folks who are no longer with us and are so sorely missed. It brought those days back to me so vividly and made me realize how truly blessed I was to be associated with that great show and all those special people. It also opened my eyes to the fact that the present and future hold so many more challenges still to be met and experiences still to be savored.

I know it's finally time for me to say goodbye to *The Hollywood Squares*, but, for some reason, I still find that difficult to do. Maybe I'll just take one more cue from the show and say—it's a wrap.

Index of Names